FERNAND DACQUIN

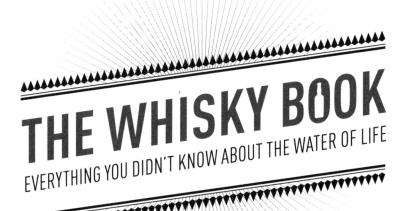

THE WHISKY BOOK

EVERYTHING YOU DIDN'T KNOW ABOUT THE WATER OF LIFE

Lannoo

PREFACE

BY THE EARL OF ERROLL, CHIEF OF CLAN HAY,
A PATRON OF THE KEEPERS OF THE QUAICH

The author first came to my house in Sandy in 2012. I was told that previously he had been a Flemish travel journalist, with a keen interest in Scotland, Scottish history and, in particular, Scotch whiskies.

There were other people invited that day and I noticed that he was not looking to converse right away. He was more interested in exploring my house. He was taking pictures of my collection of antique whisky hip flasks, and of a chessboard where each piece carries the coat of arms of one of my ancestors on its shield. It was obvious that he was looking for little stories. I was only able to attract his attention when I showed him the whisky bar, hidden in the wall of the library.

These days there are many books about whisky. That's because there are countless tales of whisky woven through our history, in the lives of people ordinary and famous, often embedded in small events, many that have never been told. We must cherish those stories. They enrich our whisky tradition.

Fernand Dacquin travelled the world for forty years writing for a tourism magazine and for whisky magazines. Wherever he went he collected anecdotes, facts, and stories about whisky. Given its rich whisky heritage, Scotland was a recurrent theme in all of this. From his copious collection of travel notes he distilled about a hundred short whisky stories. They are bundled into this book.

When the Dutch edition was published in 2020, Charles MacLean wrote the following in his preface:

"The topics Fernand has chosen to write about in this book are staggeringly eclectic and born of his own global travels: entertaining, surprising, informative (I learned a lot!), and opinionated (in a gentle way!)." I don't know what else can be added to that.

It is a bounteous book that you can dip into, starting and finishing on any page. Because of its compact size, an added bonus is that you always have a hand free for a wee dram.

I have no hesitation in recommending this book to every whisky lover, and especially to those who love a good yarn.

CONTENTS

WHISKY OR WHISKEY?

WHAT A MESS

Long ago, everything was much simpler. There was a rule that was easy to remember: countries with an 'e' in their name wrote 'whiskey' with an 'e'; countries without 'e' in their name stuck to 'whisky', without the 'e'.

Ireland? Whiskey.

Canada? Whisky.

United States? Whiskey.

Scotland? Whisky.

Simple.

But today you have to travel across the entire world map to find a country where no one produces 'whiskey'. Or 'whisky'. And those newcomers apparently really enjoy writing 'whisky' today and 'whiskey' the next day. They don't care at all!

Not all whisky is whisky.

But I'm in trouble: how can I write a book about whisky if I don't know whether it's 'whisky' or 'whiskey'?

And who is responsible for this nonsense?

Time for a serious investigation.

Bring out the musty history books.

By 1965, we read, the Irish whisky industry had fallen to such a low level that only a handful of distilleries remained. They united and founded the 'Irish Distillers'. The Irish Distillers opted for the slogan 'Strong together', and to make this clear they introduced a few 'specialties' that would surprise the Scots, who were still doing well. From now on the Irish Distillers would distill three times instead of twice (the Scottish way), they would never use peat, and they would write 'whiskey' everywhere instead of 'whisky'.

So that's where it all started.

But wait, not too fast!

Let's go further back in time.

Around 1900, there was a lot of controversy around the whole 'whisky' business in the United Kingdom.

First of all: there was no law which offered a real definition of the product 'whisky' and a lot of questions arose regarding those names that were used: for example, was blended whisky also 'whisky'? So King Edward VII set up a commission. On March 2, 1908, the committee issued a report and minutes entitled 'Inquiry on Whiskey and other Potable Spirits'. Everyone in the UK was required to follow those guidelines. Whiskey was written with 'e' throughout the whole text.

Waw!

Whiskey, with an 'e'. In Scotland and in Ireland!

One year later a new release was published, and the annoying 'e' had disappeared everywhere.

Everywhere 'whisky'. No 'e' in Scotland and no 'e' in Ireland.

And since then, things went completely off track.

Some Irish kept using the 'e'. Some emigrated to America where they introduced the 'e'. But there were others already doing without 'e' because they had taken it over from the Scots and the Canadians, who adhered to the Scottish spelling: without 'e'. The 'e' slowly became more common in the States, but there are still American distillers who don't use an 'e'.

And believe me, not all are consistent in Ireland either. Paddy for example: sometimes with an 'e'; sometimes without.

And then there are some distillers in Canada...

Enough! Stop!

We will stick to 'whisky' but switch to 'whiskey' where it is more convenient.

In Dutch, there is even a word for a small whisky: 'whiskytje'. But that is complete nonsense. Every whisky lover knows that there is no such thing. All whiskies are small whiskies.

2

LINDORES ABBEY
THANKS TO DEAR OLD BROTHER JOHN COR

*'By order of the king, eight bolls of malt
for Brother John Cor to make aqua vitae.'*

Had no one ever found that little phrase in the Scottish Exchequer Rolls of 1495 (the King's annual financial report), Lindores Abbey would likely have been lost in history.

By 'the King', the writer refers to James IV, who we know was a very moderate drinker. 'Brother John Cor' refers to the brewer-distiller at Lindores Abbey, and with eight 'bolls of malt', that diligent brother is said to have been able to distill about 250 litres of alcohol (according to experts): *aqua vitae*.

And that *aqua vitae*, or 'water of life', would have been called "whisky" today.

Not bad as a stock.

🍶 Was Brother Cor's still here?

Founded in the twelfth century, the sprawling Abbey was on the edge of what is now the village of Newburgh in Fife. At that time, this was a wooded area on the little Pow stream which sprang from Lindores Loch and flowed through the Abbey, into the river Tay. There was plenty of water in the Abbey. Fantastic for brewing or distilling.

The twenty founders of the Abbey came from Kelso and were part of the Order of Tiron. The Abbey grew fast to just over thirty members. They were the so-called 'black' brothers, because of their black habits. In the same 'Scottish Exchequer Rolls', John Cor is referred to once more for his ordering of black fabric for making habits. Cor was seemingly important in Lindores Abbey. And not only for the booze.

The Abbey was prominent and influential. Important guests such as Kings Alexander III and Edward I stayed there. As did John Balliol, William Wallace, and Mary Queen of Scots.

In the sixteenth century, Scotland had a very turbulent history: Reformation supplanted the Roman Catholic faith and the Protestants sacked the Abbey in 1543. The monks stayed in Lindores until 1584, after which the Abbey gradually fell into disrepair. At the very end, even the Abbey bell was sold to the City of Edinburgh.

Many houses in Newburgh today are built with the stones of the Abbey, and in the pubs of Newburgh you can find fine examples of these.

In 1913, John McKenzie, a diligent farmer, was able to buy the land and farm built on the ruins of the Abbey. Lindores remained in the McKenzie family from then on, eventually falling into the hands of John's great-grandson Drew and Drew's younger brother Robbie.

While Robbie expanded the farm, Drew had other pursuits. For many years he was the head chef at Glenmorangie House, which belongs to and is located close to the distillery of the same name. For more than twenty years, however, he also worked on the realisation of his dream: bringing the Lindores distillery back to life.

The farm, next to the best-preserved part of the Abbey, has now been converted into a beautiful distillery with an attractive visitor centre.

Gary Haggart, former distillery manager of Diageo's Cragganmore Distillery, and his team now take care of production.

ARCHEOLOGICAL FIND?

Behind the maturing warehouses, there is a vast area that also belonged to the Abbey. There will soon be new orchards, like the ones the Abbey once had. The Order of Tiron was very skilled in agriculture and fruit growing but was also at home in the world of herbs and medicine.

Many remains of the Abbey were found during the excavation work, which was necessary for the construction of the distillery, including a dug and stone-finished ditch to ensure that water was diverted from the Pow to the Abbey. And right there, in the middle of the construction heap, the workers uncovered a large stone and clay-finished pit in the shape of a hemisphere.

Drew McKenzie: 'Archaeologists believe that this pit may have been the home of Brother Cor's still.' If this is where Brother Cor made his *aqua vitae* more than five hundred years ago, then there is no more sacred place in the whisky world than here.

Monastic atmosphere in the distillery.

3

MUCKLE FLUGGA

THE WHISKY NOBODY KNOWS

Standing on the most northern tip of the island of Unst, you can see a steep rock rising out of the sea in front of the coast, crowned with an elegant white lighthouse: Muckle Flugga. It's the most northern tip of the UK, if we leave out that tiny rocky outcrop, Out Stack, a little farther. Muckle Flugga means 'big crag'.

The famous lighthouse builder David Stevenson was commissioned to build a lighthouse there in the 1850s. He wrote to his client after visiting the site: 'The sea around the Shetland coast makes building a lighthouse in the area impossible, impractical, dangerous, too expensive, and any ship that takes that road is mad anyway.'

The lighthouse ended up being built four years later. In 26 days, more than forty men were able to build a temporary tower, which would be replaced four years later by a much larger one. The island lost its title of 'the most northerly inhabited island in the UK' when the lighthouse was automated in 1995.

Occasionally, the name 'Muckle Flugga' was found in the whisky world, referring to a mysterious whisky that matured on the Shetlands and that no one had ever tasted. People who asked for it were looked on with pity. Everyone knew that 'Muckle Flugga' was a myth. It was just like Santa Claus and Nessie.

I went to the Shetlands in search of a bottle, but I didn't learn anything. No one had seen it before. Nobody knew where it would be stocked. No one could explain to me why whisky had to winter in this hole, exposed to the horror of the sea.

Maybe this was all a joke: describing a whisky that is completely made up and giving it the name of an inhospitable rock: Muckle Flugga.

After a while, I met someone who knew someone who claimed to have seen the bottle and knew what it said on the label. Another islander indicated that the label on the back said 'smooth, honeyed with a hint of fruit, sherry finish'.

SHETLAND WHISKY, A JOKE?

Frank and Deborah Strang bought a large plot of land with a couple of sheds on the island of Unst in a place called Saxa Vord in 2007. You can't find Saxa Vord on any map. The Royal Air Force had an extensive base here a few years ago. The Ministry of Defence left for a better location.

If the Strangs hadn't built a resort around them, the sheds would have been dead by now. In addition, they also started a micro-brewery, Valhalla Brewery, in one of those vacant buildings. They now brew quite a nice beer there.

Yet another shed was converted into a true distillery. The space is large enough to hold ten stills, but there is only one lonely still in a corner. The still can only hold 500 litres, but it works. Just not in a hurry.

Does the whisky from the Shetlands mature here? ♦

Stuart Nickerson, the man who restarted the Glenglassaugh distillery in Portsoy (Aberdeenshire) in 2008, was approached to come to Unst. In 2013, together with the Strang family, he immediately set up the Shetland Distillery Company. Shetland Reel Whisky was born.

They weren't the first to do so! In 2002 the Blackwood Distillers were founded in London. They planned to build a distillery in the Shetlands. They wanted a distillery in Catfirth on the main island but changed their minds and focused on Unst. In the meantime, they produced gin in England and created their own blended malt: Muckle Flugga whisky!

In 2008 Blackwood was bankrupt. The distillery was never built.

The proposed whisky plan was taken over by a new company called Catfirth. They bought all the Muckle Flugga whisky that was wintering 'somewhere'.

Cost per barrel: one thousand pounds.

Things didn't go well for Catfirth either. The company ceased to exist in 2014.

But the Muckle Flugga is still on the market. There is also a single malt on the market. Both contain malts from Speyside. But no one knows which distilleries.

🍶 You really have to taste it.

That is a big secret.

Originally, the label stated that the whisky wintered in a cave on Unst. That term has now been replaced by 'in a hidden location'. No one in the Shetlands knows where this could be.

But if you taste the whisky, you don't care. Because it's delicious.

DU KANG
THE GOD OF WHISKY (AND THE REST)

According to Chinese and Japanese folklore, Du Kang is the god of all the spirits. That's great for us whisky drinkers, because we don't have a 'whisky god'.

Young Du Kang was working as a shepherd and one day he left his bamboo container of rice along the way. He found his tube a few days later and discovered that the rice had fermented. He came up with the idea of making a pot of alcohol out of it. Chinese people consider Du Kang to be the inventor of distillation and the father of all distillates because they believe he was the first to do it.

There is no Chinese person who can tell you how he went from shepherd to god.

They are also not entirely sure whether he actually lived, despite the fact that he is mentioned in writings from the second and third centuries.

He is said to have had a son named Heita, thought to be the inventor of vinegar.

This vinegar discovery was also by accident. Heita hid one of his father's barrels but couldn't remember where he had dropped it. When he discovered it again, the liquor had turned to vinegar.

It's understandable that Heita isn't considered a god, for vinegar isn't delicious.

The image of Du Kang, on the other hand, can be found in many drinking places in China and Taiwan.

Du Kang also gained illustrious followers. Li Bai was one of them. He lived in the eighth century and on a daily basis poured himself the best spirits and wines he could find. Once he was sufficiently drunk, he wrote conversational poems, which are considered to be among the best in Chinese literature. There are more than a thousand known. One of his most famous is called 'Waking from drunkenness on a spring day.' Beautiful, isn't it?

He was a favourite of the emperor, who loved his poems. Li Bai ended his life when he walked along a creek in which the moon was reflected. His attempt to save the moon was a failure. Days later, Li Bai's body was discovered.

We also know that Jhong Kuei, a contemporary of Li Bai, was extremely gifted and had considerable scientific knowledge. Like Li Bai, he was an incorrigible drinker. Hence, his nickname: 'the drunk'. One day the emperor refused to grant him the title of 'First Scholar'. It wasn't because of his drinking. The emperor thought he was too ugly for the title. Jhong took that refusal very seriously. He died the same day, after banging his drunken head against a pole for too long.

Du Kang isn't to blame for that. Accordingly, he remains, until further notice, the god of distillation and therefore of our whisky.

5

THOU DEMON DRINK

POETRY VS ALCOHOL

William Topaz McGonagall, son of an Irish weaver, was born in 1825. He was born in Edinburgh, but, in his own words, 'born somewhere in Ireland' is said to be closer to the truth. He probably chose Edinburgh because the laws at the time were not as strict for a native Scot as they were for an Irishman.

He worked as a weaver but also tried hard as an amateur actor. He once got a part in the performance of Macbeth. 'Got' is not the right word here, because he had to pay for it. He played Macbeth himself. The public, knowing his reputation as a poor actor, came especially to see how he would mess it up. In the final scene, he had to die in the fight with Macduff, but this turned out differently. He firmly refused to die because his opponent received more applause than he did, even though Macduff shouted 'you're dead, fall down, you idiot.'

William McGonagall.

He would become famous anyway, albeit in a completely different industry: poetry.

'In the year 1877, I discovered myself to be a poet, the most important event in my life,' writes McGonagall in his memoirs.

William Topaz McGonagall was a 'teetotaler': Not a drop of alcohol ever entered his mouth. He hated whisky and anything that included alcohol. He saw how bad drink was for the people of Perth and Dundee, where he later settled. Dundee, in particular, he found to be a real place of destruction. And there he was right. At that time, alcohol consumption in the penniless town was among the highest in the entire kingdom. With all of the consequences.

He would use his literary skills to fight whisky. There are many examples that have remained. His most beloved work 'Thou Demon Drink' has sixteen stanzas, the first five I don't want to withhold from you:

Oh, thou demon Drink, thou fell destroyer;
Thou curse of society, and its greatest annoyer.
What hast thou done to society, let me think?
I answer thou hast caused the most of ills, thou demon Drink.

Thou causeth the mother to neglect her child,
Also the father to act as he were wild,
So that he neglects his loving wife and family dear,
By spending his earnings foolishly on whisky, rum and beer.

And after spending his earnings foolishly he beats his wife
The man that promised to protect her during life

> *And so the man would if there was no drink in society,*
> *For seldom a man beats his wife in a state of sobriety.*

> *And if he does, perhaps he finds his wife fou',*
> *Then that causes, no doubt, a great hullaballo;*
> *When he finds his wife drunk he begins to frown,*
> *And in a fury of passion he knocks her down.*

> *And in that knock down she fractures her head,*
> *And perhaps the poor wife she is killed dead,*
> *Whereas, if there was no strong drink to be got,*
> *To be killed wouldn't have been the poor wife's lot.*

His poems are recognisable by the lack of imagery, rhythm, and vocabulary. He used stop words when he couldn't come up with a good rhyming word. He could always rely on his audience. He liked it and he enjoyed the honour.

The greatest honour that he received was from... India. Or so he thought. He received a letter in his mailbox in December 1894.

The person who wrote it was none other than 'King Theebaw of Burmah and the Andaman Islands in India'. His Royal Highness was clearly a big fan of William's work and begged him to accept the Andaman Islands Honour Ribbon. So, he became a knight in the Holy Order of the White Elephant.

McGonagall was allowed to call himself the 'Keeper of the White Elephant' after that. He cherished this title until the end of his life.

The British students who sent the letter have never been identified.

William Topaz McGonagall died penniless on September 29, 1902, and is buried at Greyfriars Kirkyard in Edinburgh.

In the Writers' Museum in Edinburgh they want to give him a place of honour, next to Sir Walter Scott. There were even calls for his remains to be transferred to Poets' Corner in Westminster Abbey.

6

DRAMBUIE

BONNIE PRINCE CHARLES' WHISKY

The MacKinnon clan is not one of the largest in Scotland, but it has a nice history. The first King of the Picts and the first King of Scotland was Kenneth MacAlpin. It's a good start to have such an ancestor.

Throughout the history of Scotland, you will occasionally find the name MacKinnon, but it's usually not associated with the most heroic circumstances.

That is, until Bonnie Prince Charles, the most romantic figure in Scottish history, arrives on the scene. This Charles was the grandson of James VII of Scotland, who had to leave the country as a Catholic when the Reformers got the upper hand. James VII was replaced by his son-in-law, William III of Orange, a Protestant.

A couple of years later, Bonnie Prince Charles, then living in France and Italy, was convinced that he was the rightful heir to the throne of Scotland.

Strathaird and the Quillin Hills on Skye.

He was supported by many Scottish clans and followers who called themselves the Jacobite. The campaign began in the summer of 1745 and ended after a short battle in the plains at Culloden on April 16, 1746. The Jacobite were wiped out at Culloden.

Culloden marked the end for the Prince. But years later, the legendary Flora MacDonald managed to disguise Bonnie Prince Charles as her maid Betty Burke. After some island hopping, he ended up on the Isle of Skye, which was a safer place for him. He found a place to stay with John MacKinnon. Later on, John was sentenced to four years in prison for this crime, and he had to stay on a boat on the Thames.

Charles was able to flee from Skye to France, fathering an illegitimate child on the way, and travelling on to Italy. He grabbed the bottle in order to forget the whole project. He was found dead in the street many years later. The trail to the rightful Scottish King ended with him.

But he had left something in Scotland. John MacKinnon received a reward for his generosity: a note with the recipe for a whisky cocktail that is sure to make you happy: Drambuie. You pronounce this divine drink as 'drem bjoewie' and not as 'draambwie', like the French, because you can't get much more Scottish than Drambuie. The name is Gaelic and means 'the drink that satisfies you'.

Flora MacDonald's house where the prince briefly stayed..

PRINCE RECIPE

There is a mystery to how the prince came up with this recipe. Some claim it belonged to his mother, but that's nonsense. He may have taken it out of the mundane world of France, where he was regularly seen enjoying banquets and parties. The recipe was kept secret for more than 150 years by the MacKinnons. They would sometimes mix the ingredients together at home, but only for their own use and for visitors who could keep a secret. MacKinnon patented the name as a trademark in 1892. He realized there was cash in the recipe. He started in Edinburgh with the production of Drambuie. He was aware that his Drambuie was a marketing asset and knew keeping the recipe a secret was a good idea.

John MacKinnon was the only one who knew the true composition of Drambuie. It would be a tradition: in each generation of the MacKinnons, there was only one person who knew all the ingredients and how to blend them. For safety's sake, the MacKinnons put a piece of paper with the whole secret neatly written down in a safe deposit box at a notary.

At first, Malcolm MacKinnon is likely to have reached for a whisky from the island. We can only guess which one; most likely it was Talisker. But of course, there's more to Drambuie than whisky. We know several herbs are used, and heather honey. Cloves and saffron are also mentioned, but the rest remains a secret. During Prohibition in America, Drambuie made a big splash: the drink was masterful and less ostentatious to use in cocktails. The

Strathhaird.

blend of Drambuie and other whiskys was a big hit. In those sad 'non-alcoholic' years, this drink was called B.I.F. or D&S. We (and the rest of the world) now call it Rusty Nail. It's a drink that gained a lot of legendary followers, including Humphrey Bogart and Frank Sinatra.

In 2014, William Grant & Sons, who we know from Glenfiddich and The Balvenie, bought Drambuie's recipe for about one hundred million ponds. It is possible that the new owners will use their own whisky as the basis for this liqueur.

Drambuie was the first liqueur to be allowed into the venerable pantries of the House of Lords. And that is quite an honour.

7

'IF BY WHISKEY...'

THE FAMOUS WHISKEY SPEECH

Noah S. Sweat Jr. was raised in a family for whom politics were deeply ingrained. His father was a member of the US House of Representatives, and Noah Jr. was following in his footsteps. Born in 1922, he was just 24 years old when he first served as a delegate. Like his father, Noah S. Sweat Jr. would later become a judge. He died from Parkinson's in 1996.

There was a lot of turbulence in the world of alcohol in the US in the 1950s. Many states still had total or partial bans on the sale of whiskey, despite the fact that Prohibition had ended.

The legalisation of whiskey and other liqueurs was hence a daily topic of lively discussion, both in politics and on the street. The sale was legalised by the Senate, but the House of Representatives did not act on it.

Mississippi - The counties in black are dry.

On Friday, April 4, 1952, Noah Sweat Jr. was invited to speak at a banquet at the King Edward Hotel in Jackson, Mississippi. At that time, the state was still completely 'dry'. There were some exceptions for beer and light wines, subject to licenses, and spirits for religious and medical purposes. But nothing more.

Most of the audience that evening was involved in politics. As expected, the audience was mixed and consisted of both supporters and opponents of the legalisation. Sweat's speech was quite short, but very powerful. Sweat is said to have worked on it for a long time.

The newspaper *The Clarion-Ledger* reported, the day after the lecture: 'The room was completely silent during the first half of the speech, followed by a "tremendous burst of applause" at the end.'

THE WHISKEY SPEECH

My friends,

I had not intended to discuss this controversial subject at this particular time. However, I want you to know that I do not shun controversy. On the contrary, I will take a stand on any issue at any time, regardless of how fraught with controversy it might be. You have asked me how I feel about whiskey. All right, here is how I feel about whiskey.

If when you say 'whiskey' you mean the devil's brew, the poison scourge, the bloody monster, that defiles innocence, dethrones reason, destroys the home, creates misery and poverty, yea, literally takes the bread from the mouths of little children; if you mean the evil drink that topples the Christian man and woman from the pinnacle of righteous, gracious living into the bottomless pit of degradation and despair and shame and helplessness and hopelessness, then certainly I am against it.

But if when you say 'whiskey' you mean the oil of conversation, the philosophic wine, the ale that is consumed when good fellows get together, that puts a song in their hearts and laughter on their lips, and the warm glow of contentment in their eyes; if you mean Christmas cheer; if you mean the stimulating drink that puts the spring in the old gentleman's step on a frosty, crispy morning; if you mean the drink which enables a man to magnify his joy, and his happiness, and to forget, if

This is what you do with confiscated whiskey.

only for a little while, life's great tragedies, and heartaches, and sorrows; if you mean that drink, the sale of which pours into our treasuries untold millions of dollars, which are used to provide tender care for our little crippled children, our blind, our deaf, our dumb, our pitiful aged and infirm, to build highways and hospitals and schools, then certainly I am for it.

This is my stand. I will not retreat from it. I will not compromise.

Noah Spurgeon Sweat Jr.'s speech is still considered the most important speech from the Prohibition era today. The term 'if-by-whiskey' now refers to a delivery style that introduces ambiguity into a discussion.

Mississippi would remain completely 'dry' until 1966.

Noah S. Sweat Jr. was later nicknamed 'Soggy', because of his haircut, which apparently impressed the audience as much as his speech.

8

BORVO
GALLIC GOD OF WHISKEY

You can find a well that is sadly dry in the main street of the Gallic settlement of Bibracte in France. A solid wall was built around it to collect the water, but it stands today aimlessly.

The rich and poor Gauls who lived here loved this sparkling water. They believed that the god Borvo was responsible for it. If there was a new well found in Gaul, the Gauls immediately attributed it to Borvo. This 'god of sparkling waters' looked after the physical and spiritual well-being of every Gaul. You can bathe in it, but also drink it. 'Borvo water is water of life' might have been their advertising slogan.

The Battle of Long Island.

The well is the place of pilgrimage for Borvo's followers.

There were other places where Borvo was popular. The name Borvo was projected into all the places where Borvo was worshiped by the French. They referred to him not as Borvo but as 'Bourbon', pronounced 'bour-bon'. The word is now found in many place names like Bourbonne-les-Bains and Bourbonnais.

Louis XVI, le Roi-Martyr, was the last reigning king of the French House of Bourbon. That name was derived from the castle Bourbon-l'Archambault. The royal house produced many kings, but they disappeared after the French Revolution in 1789. A mock trial found Louis XVI guilty of high treason and sentenced him to death. He was guillotined, earning the unenviable title of 'the only executed French king.'

Ten years earlier and thousands of miles to the west, the English had their hands full with the uprising in the colonies of what is now the United States. There was a war of independence from 1775 to 1783. Louis XIV thought that he should support the colonies. As a Frenchman, he could hardly pass up such a great opportunity to fool the English.

As we know, the English had to retreat and the colonies became independent. To demonstrate their gratitude to the French, the Americans renamed part of Fayette County in Virginia 'Bourbon County'. From now on, we should pronounce Bourbon as "beu-bn" instead of "bour-bon".

Kentucky County, Virginia, was established in 1776. It was split into three counties after four years. One was Fayette County, Virginia. In 1785, part of Fayette County was transformed into a new county: Bourbon County, Virginia. In 1792 a new state was formed, the 15th in the USA: the state of Kentucky. To make that possible, a great part of Bourbon County, Virginia, was transferred to the new state and divided into counties, one of which is what we now call Bourbon County, Kentucky.

However, the old area is still referred to as Old Bourbon. And Old Bourbon was also mentioned on the barrels of whiskey that were produced and traded there. Quite misleading, because the word 'old' immediately suggests years of aging to whiskey lovers, not the case here. Perhaps that's why references were made to the contents of the barrels, without mentioning "old": it stayed with "bourbon".

THE GENTLEMAN DISTILLERY

During the early 1800s, a lot of alcohol was produced in the US. More than a hundred distilleries were in full operation in Old Bourbon. There was a lot of drinking as well. But the time was near for prohibition. There was considerable opposition to the disastrous effects of excessive alcohol consumption, and some states enacted strict laws. By 1850, twelve states were completely dry.

In 1919, the Volstead Act would herald the start of a unique period for the entire US, which began in 1920 and would last until 1933: a complete prohibition. The Americans ran out of booze, or at least that was the intention. However, Section 7 of the Act stated that '... no one but a physician holding a permit to prescribe liquor shall issue any prescription for liquor.'

In Bourbon County, only six distilleries were allowed to continue operating, solely for medical purposes. Prohibition came to an end in December 1933. There were 282,122 illegal distilleries discovered afterwards.

In Bourbon County, production came to a complete stop, and there were no distilleries left. Contrary to popular belief, Bourbon is not a 'dry county' because alcohol can be freely sold there.

🌢 Pernicious whiskey under lock and key.

In 2004, 95 years after the start of Prohibition, Andrew and Larissa Buchanan started a new small distillery in Paris, Kentucky, the capital of Bourbon County.

They picked the name 'The Gentleman'. It was already used by colleagues, so it was not a good choice. Now the business is called Hartfield & Co, referring to their distant ancestors who came over from Germany and started a distillery around 1800. Their story ended with a fire, but their descendants brought Bourbon Whiskey to the market.

MARTIN MARTIN
THE FATHER OF THE FIRST 'TASTING NOTES'

Born in the second half of the seventeenth century on the Isle of Skye, Martin Martin is the author of two significant books: 'A voyage to St Kilda' and 'A Description of the Western Isles of Scotland'. The works are important because they are among the first descriptions of a completely unknown part of Scotland.

Martin had an advantage over a few others who had preceded him on those islands: he was able to communicate with the inhabitants because he spoke the language of the islands: Gaelic.

He described exactly what he heard and saw, without the artificial romanticism that authors after him liked to add. In addition, Martin was well educated. He studied art and humanities at the University of Edinburgh and medicine in Leiden, becoming familiar with a lot of influential people in the process.

A

DESCRIPTION

OF THE

𝔚𝔢𝔰𝔱𝔢𝔯𝔫 𝔍𝔰𝔩𝔞𝔫𝔡𝔰

OF

SCOTLAND.

CONTAINING

A Full Account of their Situation, Extent, Soils, Product, Harbours, Bays, Tides, Anchoring-Places, and Fisheries.

The Antient and Modern Government, Religion and Customs of the Inhabitants ; particularly of their Druids, Heathen Temples, Monasteries, Churches, Chappels, Antiquities, Monuments, Forts, Caves, and other Curiosities of Art and Nature : Of their Admirable and Expeditious Way of Curing most Diseases by Simples of their own Product.

A Particular Account of the *Second Sight*, or Faculty of foreseeing things to come, by way of Vision, so common among them.

A Brief Hint of Methods to improve Trade in that Country, both by Sea and Land.

With a New MAP of the Whole, describing the Harbours, Anchoring-Places, and dangerous Rocks, for the benefit of Sailors.

To which is added, A Brief Description of the Isles of *Orkney* and *Schetland.*

By *M. MARTIN*, Gent.

The SECOND EDITION, very much Corrected.

LONDON,

Printed for A. BELL at the Cross-Keys and Bible in *Cornhill*; T. VARNAM and J. OSBORN in *Lombard-street*; W. TAYLOR at the Ship, and J. BAKER and T. WARNER at the Black Boy in *Paternoster-Row.* M. DCC. XVI.

Martin Martin's 'masterpiece'.

fore, occasions several Disorders in those who eat the Bread, or drink the Ale made of that Corn ; such as the Head-ach and Vomiting.

THE Natives are very industrious, and undergo a great Fatigue by digging the Ground with Spades, and in most places they turn the Ground so digged upside down, and cover it with Sea-ware; and in this manner there are about 500 People employ'd daily for some months. This way of labouring is by them call'd *Timiy*; and certainly produces a greater Increase than digging or plowing otherwise. They have little Harrows with wooden Teeth in the first and second Rows, which break the Ground ; and in the third Row they have rough Heath, which smooths it. This light Harrow is drawn by a Man having a strong Rope of Horse-hair across his Breast.

THEIR plenty of Corn was such, as dispos'd the Natives to brew several sorts of Liquors, as common *Usquebaugh*, another call'd *Trestarig, id est, Aqua-vitæ*, three times distill'd, which is strong and hot ; a third sort is four times distill'd, and this by the Natives is call'd *Usquebaugh-baul, id est, Usquebaugh,* which at first taste affects all the Members of the Body : two spoonfuls of this last Liquor is a sufficient Dose; and if any Man exceed this, it would presently stop his Breath, and endanger his Life. The *Trestarig* and *Usquebaugh-baul,* are both made of Oats.

But his books were not high-quality literary gems, as Samuel Johnson suggested, reading them half a century later: "No one has ever been as bad at writing as Martin Martin." But they are meritorious contributions because they are almost the only sources that give us a glimpse of life on those islands around 1695.

The vast majority of the two books describe the customs of the people, their diet and manners, their eating and drinking, their few contacts with the outside world, their beliefs and superstitions, their dangers, diseases, and remedies, and their contacts with witches and ghosts and other strange happenings. For instance: Martin described meeting a blind man on Harris who was still able to see during a full moon. The author also learned that cuckoos on St Kilda only appear on the days when an important visitor arrives on the island, or when an important person dies.

USQUEBAUGH-BAUL

In the midst of this metaphysical wisdom, we discover that: 'On the Isle of Harris, the air is temperately cold and the natives endeavour to qualify it by taking a dose of *aqua vitae*, or brandy, for they brew no such liquors as trestarig and usquebaugh-baul!' Fortunately, Martin explains more about this in other places.

On his visit to the Isle of Lewis, we were given the first lesson in the art of distilling. 'Their plenty of corn on Lewis was such as disposed the residents to brew several sorts of liquors as common usquebaugh, another called "trestarig", which is an *aqua vitae* that has been distilled three times, which is strong and hot. A third variety is four times distilled. The natives call it "usquebaugh-baul", which is Gaelic and means "dangerous whisky", which at first taste affects all the members of the body.'

Two tablespoons of it were recommended as the maximum dose. If you take more of it, Martin wrote, you'd risk your breathing stopping immediately. 'Trestarig' and 'usquebaugh-baul' were both made from oats.These texts might be called the 'oldest known tasting notes'.

Three hundred years later, Jim McEwan, at that time the legendary master distiller at Bruichladdich, drew on Martin Martin's work to create his unique 'X4 whisky'; the 'only' whisky distilled four times.

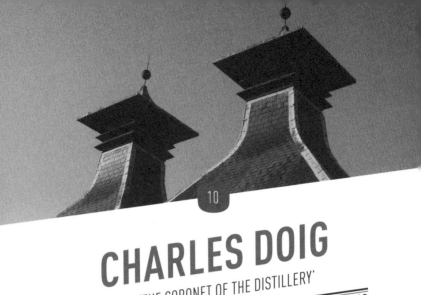

CHARLES DOIG
AND 'THE CORONET OF THE DISTILLERY'

10

Charles Doig, the son of a farmer from the Scottish region of Angus, born in 1855, excelled at school.

He was particularly drawn towards sciences and he excelled in mathematics. He left school when he was fifteen years old. Doig was hired by John Carver, an architect from the area, and given *carte blanche* to design and sketch.

In 1880, Doig married Margaret Dick, and moved with her to Elgin, in the heart of Speyside. He was hired at the successful surveying company H.M.S. Mackay, at the time a successful business.

Charles was enthusiastic about the job. He convinced his employer that he was a valuable designer in his own right. Marius Mackay suggested that he join the business, and Charles

Glenfiddich.

did it right away. The next step was not easy, but Charles Doig took over the company after just a few years.

He immediately focused on the whisky industry. Existing distilleries dreamed of renewal and expansion, while new distilleries were launched. Doig had already worked for several distilleries at Mackay. But it would take until around 1890 for him to introduce the greatest innovation in whisky production: the pagoda.

The assignment came from Thomas Mackenzie, one of the owners of the Dailuaine Distillery. (Pronounced dall-joe-an, with the stress on the second syllable). The distillery is still operational today and is owned by Diageo, one of the largest producers of spirits and beer in the world. A lot of distilleries remain in business by producing malt alcohol for the blends of this giant multinational. There aren't many bottles of Dailuaine single malt on the market.

One of the problems that Mackenzie needed solving related to the discharge of the smoke in the kilns when drying the green malt. Doig was used to drawing buildings, stills, and mash tuns, but he had never encountered a problem like this before.

DOIG PAGODE

Nevertheless, Charles Doig redesigned the chimney cap over Dailuaine's kiln, shaping it in such a thoughtful (and elegant) way that the entire smoke evacuation effect of the chimney was maximized.

It was a 'miracle' that did not go under the radar. The news spread so quickly that many distilleries wanted a 'Doig fan' like the one at Dailuaine. The expression 'Doig pagoda' did not appear as a technical term until much later.

The first Doig Pagoda was destroyed in the Dailuaine Distillery fire in 1917, a year before the death of its founder. Meanwhile, many other distilleries installed Doig fans, not only because of the positive effects on production but also because the 'pagoda' had gradually become the symbol of the entire whisky industry. After Doig's death, the distilleries were still loyal to his fan. Doig was involved in the planning and construction of 56 Scottish distilleries. Those on a tour of Scotland today and seeking out distilleries are looking for those mini-roofs.

Ardbeg.

Ask anyone to sketch a distillery and the pagoda will not be missing. Only a small number of Scottish distilleries still malt their own barley, using the kiln. The hassle of malting is labour intensive. Industrial malthouses can now supply the malt on demand, according to customers' wishes.

Distilleries that still work with a malt floor do it mainly for the tourists.

But while the kiln and malt floor disappeared (or became a visitor centre), the pagoda held firm. Not only in Scotland, but also in many new whisky countries such as Taiwan and South Africa.

The architecture of the most modern distilleries often overlooks the pagoda and many 'sensitive' whisky enthusiasts look on with sorrow.

EENDRACHT MAAKT WHISKY

COBURG 1830. DE EERSTE BELGISCHE SINGLE MALT.

Dufftown in de Schotse Highlands, 18 oktober 1968.

Tijdens een werkbezoek aan de whiskydistilleerderij van Martin Corrigan ontmoet **Anne Reserve**, geneversmaker van vader op zoon, her uit de streek van Wortegem **Serge de Ryverseh**, een 30 jaar jonge, ondernemende telg uit een oud geslacht van likeurstokers uit Sint-Amore in het Luiksie.

Zowel elke historische ontmoeting zal ook deze niet toevallig blijken.

Reeds enkele jaren doorkruisen beide distilleerders immers Schotland van noord naar zuid om er zich de **eeuwenoude geheimen van het whiskystoken** eigen te maken.

Tot hun verbazing ontdekken ze dat ze dezelfde excentrieke ambitie koesteren: een **Belgische whisky** stoken die de vergelijking met de beste Schotse whisky zonder te wanhelen kan doorstaan.

Het klikt meteen tussen de beide enthousiaste stokers die nog diezelfde avond langdurig rond de tafel gaan zitten, met in hun midden nog de geur van **de smeulende turf** waarmee **Martin Corrigan**, zoals de Keltische monniken eeuwen terug, de kiemende gerstekorrels droogstookt.

Er wordt uitvoerig geproefd en ondanks de taalbarrières (en dankzij de whisky van Martin) ziek steeds vlotter gepraat, steeds stouter gedroomd.

Wanneer die 19de oktober bij het krieken van de dag **Reserve** en **de Ryversch** met een licht Schots...

...accent afscheid nemen van elkaar, is de **Coburg 1830, de eerste Belgische single malt whisky**, een feit dat name staat dan de dooreen. Nehie op dat een van de dag.

Terug in België lopen **Reserve** en **de Ryversch** in Molenbeek een oude stokerij op die ze zo-het tot meer klaarstomen voor productie. Mooita noch techniek worden gespaard. Authentieke, koperen alambieken (de befaamde **pot stills**), importeren geïmporteerd uit Groenten den en hun aldoorge-bullgien met verbiebas van de Schotse Highlands naar de Molenbuchse stokerij. In de Spaanse bodega's worden honderden **oude sherryvaten in Amerikaanse eik** uit na vat zorgvuldig geselecteerd. Daaruit zal steeds de eerste **Coburg 1830** zijn bijzondere aroma en dieps gouddkleur puren. Twaalf stille jaren lang.

Reserve en de Ryversch proeven die dagen voor water dan goed is voor whiskykenners. Als lange-wijde '**sings beusha**' stekers wijzen ze immers dat alles ontstaan uit water, das ook de whisky. Ze tasten unnienken voor het nachts water van **de Hoge Venen**, soepel en levendig en mee die subtiele turfsmaak die mee wat zwaarder singlie malt whisky zo onnoemend maakt.

De geest wordt uit de polders onze eigen laaglands aangevoerd. Nergens anders vinden ze hem voller, dropter en zoeter.

Op 1 oktober 1986 bereiken komt **Martin Buchanan**, 55 jaar oud, 44 jaar in het vak en ge-rejpuneerd 'stillman' (meester...

...distilleerder) uit Schotland, het zieverschin on engvoldige toon zal in hun stokerij verrengen. Het stoken kan beginnen.

Wie die midernie in de buurt van de **Coburg 1830** opheft komt, wordt aangenaam verrast door de overnge turfgeur die de Molenbeekse lucht ruim een week lang gijsdt. Of door drie uit het gizvalde nekbleutelse toon dat de stokerij 2 dagen en nachten op haar oude gwerstemen doordovevn, veugeleverd aan de niebeterhouse byschten van een **eeuwde alchimie**.

Op 11 november 1989 kan de eerste **Coburg 1830**, de vereste genuine Belgian made club whisky een **zwaalfjarige sleep begurinen**.

Sindus al en ton gwoerd door de schaalende suvnanpjen en de tijdenloize idee van **Reserve** en **de Ryversch** die, als het hen echt te sterk wordt, zu nen verbldogsuthe het tijpende droom komen bevinden.

Vandnag zijn Anne Reserve en Serge de Ryversch bijzonder trots.

De **Coburg 1830**, hun Belgische single malt whisky lijkt een eigen-zinnige en hoogstandige whisky te zijn die hun oorzaste verwachtingen ver overtreft. Zeldzaam gezofisticeerd met een vraig geraffineerd, een rijk en fruitig aroma en een lichte turfsmaak die doel overlook met een experience bliep of een Campbeltown whisky.

Trots zijn ze tol onder uit, de een wel smvge Vlaamse, de andere een keppige Waal, met hun Belgische **Coburg 1830** gainklidweg hebben aangetoond dat eendracht inerweer renminsten ukwetet dan erzijd. Iur het transsder is whisky te stoken dan mute.

11

COBURG 1830
THE 'FIRST' BELGIAN WHISKY

A colourful full-page advertisement appeared in all Belgian newspapers on March 11, 1999. In both the Dutch and French languages. They brought out the good news: a twelve-year-old single malt was to be marketed in Belgium. The very first whisky 'made in Belgium': a whisky called Coburg 1830.

The bottle could not have been more Belgian. The headline referred to the Belgian national motto: 'Eendracht maakt macht' ('Unity gives strength'). A three-colored ribbon ran from top to bottom: black, yellow, and red. Belgium's national colours were repeated all over the bottle.

The name of the whisky spoke volumes: '1830' was the year of Belgian independence, and 'Coburg' referred to the Royal House: Saxe-Coburg and Gotha. (After the First World War, the descendants changed their name wisely to 'from Belgium'.)

It was a somewhat odd combination. The brand new country, Belgium, made no mention of the Coburgs. At the time, the Belgians were still combing through foreign nobility,

Coburg whiskies are 'real'.

looking for someone who would dare become king of this IKEA buffer state, wedged between a few superpowers. Leopold I accepted the job only a year later and arrived in Belgium as late as July 1831.

The sight of the glass in the ad must have caused any experienced single-malt connoisseurs shiver. They had thrown two huge chunks of ice in what they claimed was a unique, taste-rich malt whisky. Ice, in a single malt! And the glass was such that you would only pour a gooey liqueur for someone you disliked. And then there was the text.

The distillery, located in Molenbeek, was launched by a Flemish woman from Wortegem and a young Walloon man from Stoumont. 'Unity', you know. They met in 1985 at a distillery in Dufftown, Scotland, 'by the smell of peat, the distiller used to dry his barley'. They produced the first spirit on November 11th (a national holiday). The barley they used came from the polders, in the west of the country, where the soil is generally too heavy for that purpose.

Yet many readers (and also some whisky connoisseurs) fell for it. The ad cost five million Belgian francs (200,000 euros) and was seen by more than 4,272,000 readers. More than 30,000 people responded by phone because they were offered a chance to win a bottle of Coburg 1830. But the Coburg 1830 whisky was a complete fake.

SAATCHI & SAATCHI

The advertisement had been created by the renowned advertising agency Saatchi & Saatchi, on behalf of two advertising agencies, Full Page and Scripta. They wanted to prove that advertising in newspapers worked. The names of the 'founders' of the distillery in Molenbeek were anagrams of the names of the two bosses of Full Page and Scripta.

Readers could win a bottle by calling a pay phone number, paying eighteen francs (50 euro cents) per minute. The proceeds were donated to charity. Five hundred callers were drawn by lot and received a bottle. But many companies also received a package with a bottle, to further highlight that advertising in newspapers was important.

But if Coburg 1830 didn't exist, what was in that bottle?

THE CONTENT COUNTS

The European Regulation 110 of 2008 defines the term 'whisky' strictly. Each Member State was obliged to transpose that regulation and definition into national law. So you can't just put 'whisky' on a bottle if the content does not meet the many points from that definition. Let's take a look at the Coburg 1830 bottle. We assume that the front of the bottle was intended to be an eye-catching feature. We need to look at the back.

The small label on the back is a bit more honest. It literally says: Single malt Scotch whisky – 3 years old. So the 'twelve years' on the front was also a lie. Below, in small print: 'Bottled by Koninks, Zonhoven, Belgium, importers of Speyburn whisky.' I would be happy to give it a chance.

W.C. FIELDS
DRINKING FOR JOKE

You'll agree with me. It's difficult to make friends when you throw out bothersome one-liners.

'I don't drink anything stronger than gin before breakfast.'

'A woman drove me to drink, and I didn't even have the decency to thank her.'

'I'm not prejudiced, I hate everyone equally.'

But William Claude Dunkenfield, better known as W.C. Fields, was able to get away with it. The life story of the most quoted creator of alcohol aphorisms is full of lies and inventions, mostly perpetrated by himself. For instance, he was fond of questioning whether his name was Dunkenfield or Dunkinfield. He appropriated a number of different pseudonyms: Figley B. Whitesides, Docter Opis Guelpe, Felton J. Satchelstern, Mahatma Kane Jeeves, Otis

W.C. Fields.

Criblecoblis, and many others. There are three versions of his date of birth that he has thrown around, but it's assumed he was born in 1880. He went to school until he was eight and then ran away from home because his alcoholic father beat him up when he helped him to sell vegetables on the street.

W.C. Fields grew up in Philadelphia, a city he would hate all his life. He managed to express his 'affection' for it briefly in statements: "I was once in Philadelphia for a whole year, I believe it was on a Sunday.' Another: 'I went to Philadelphia, it was closed.' He didn't want to be buried there either.

As a small boy, he had mastered juggling and he demonstrated his skill at every turn. He began performing as a street performer, and soon became known, eventually becoming a sought-after variety star. He performed in Europe, Asia, Australia, and the United States. Queen Victoria and other Royals would enjoy his performances.

He never spoke during those performances. Unless something went wrong. Then one of his assistants was subject to his rage.

He appeared on posters of the Folies Bergères in Paris, Ziegfeld Follies in New York, and many others. It was in New York that he entered the film world. He shot his first film in 1915, but it took another ten years before his breakthrough.

At Ziegfeld he met a lovely woman named Bessie Pool. She was one of the many 'Ziegfeld beauties'. She bore him a son in 1927. He also had a mistress at the time, the Mexican Carlotta Monti, who knew nothing about his affair with Bessie, and even less about the fact that he had been married to Harriet Hughes since 1900, who had taught him to read and write and with whom he also had a son, born in 1904.

ALCOHOLIC OR NOT?

Anyone who encountered W.C. Fields might have immediately believed they had a drunk in front of them. His swollen, red nose and drunken voice gave that impression. The nose was actually a relic of a street fight, and his raspy voice was the result of the many throat infections he had contracted as a child, often sleeping in damp rooms. But that voice would

Fields lends a hand in 'You Can't Cheat an Honest Man'.

become part of his success, especially as a ventriloquist.

Alcohol came later in his life. There is no juggler who can afford trembling hands and so whisky and gin weren't on William's agenda. He hated having to work with people who had been drinking. In the last ten years of his life, however, Fields began reaching for the bottle. Around 1940, he suffered strong bouts of delirium tremens.

In the meantime, he spread untruths about himself with crazy statements. Did he really hate children and dogs? Did he mean it when he said: 'all women are crazy, the difference is only in the degree'?

Was his statement correct: 'I spent half my money on gambling, alcohol and wild women. The other half I wasted'?

The facts do not suggest so. He had many happy relationships. He was fond of clowning around with children when they came to visit. He even founded an institution for orphans with his own money. There was a strict condition in his institution: no religion could be taught.

He disliked religion. Yet a friend caught him reading the Bible on his last sickbed. 'I'm just checking for escape routes!' he is reported to have said.

He died in 1946, on Christmas Day, the holiday he hated all his life.

BIAWA MAKALUNGA
THE 'SPIRIT' OF ROTHES

The second Matabele War, at the end of the nineteenth century, took place in what is now Zimbabwe. During the war, a baby was abandoned under a bush, along a road which had just been passed by a British column.

The baby was noticed by Major James Grant, a native of Rothes in Speyside, Scotland. He sheltered the child and immediately came up with a name: Biawa. He brought the child to Scotland after the war ended in 1902.

The foundling was a welcome figure in the village and grew up to be a strong man. He worked as a servant for the Grants and became a famous football player. The local soccer team was very happy to have him.

The Glenrothes Distillery isn't in Glenrothes, but in Rothes, two hundred miles to the north. If you enquire in Rothes about the Glenrothes Distillery, there's a good chance they'll look at you with questioning eyes.

The distillery seems to be a well-kept secret. But if you ask for the local cemetery, you will find it automatically.

A narrow street leads you along a side arm of the Spey to the cemetery and the street suddenly ends there... in the distillery. The distillery overlooks a hill covered with gravestones. They are coloured black because of the alcohol-loving fungus found on the walls of the distillery and on the buildings in the area.

One tombstone, on top of the hill, says simply 'Biawa'. At the bottom of the stone we find the year of his death: 1972.

In 1979 Glenrothes installed new stills in the distillery. After the work was done, the hazy outline of a mysterious figure suddenly appeared in the 'stillroom': a black man with a whitish-grey beard. The strange man was seen again by night shift workers a few days later. He appeared to be very restless. And so it continued. He would often wander between the stills, but was most commonly seen sitting next to the entrance of the still room. He usually disappeared as quickly as he appeared, but did not always stay for long.

The distillery manager was not very happy about it and called on Cedric Wilson. An outstanding mathematician and a specialist in supernatural

Spirits on both sides of the street.

phenomena, this university professor was also an outstanding teacher. After careful investigation, he concluded that the new stills and excavations had disrupted the earth's rays passing beneath the distillery.

He said that it could be very inconvenient for ghosts. He went to the cemetery immediately, walked slowly between the graves and then stopped at one. Bystanders watched him engage in a lengthy and gesture-filled conversation. When the professor returned, he said that his conversation had been fruitful and that an agreement had been struck with the ghost: it was time to stop digging.

The grave belonged to Biawa Makalunga, who had died seven years earlier.

Since then, Biawa Makalunga has not been seen. The respect for his spirit has not changed.

Nowadays, many people in Rothes drink the first whisky of the day as a 'toast to Biawa'.

14

JESSIE COWAN

THE SCOTTISH MOTHER OF JAPANESE WHISKY

One day a young Japanese man knocked at the door of Dr. Cowan's house in Kirkintilloch, a town near Glasgow. He asked if a room was still available to rent. Jessie Cowan, whom everyone called Rita, might have been at the piano at that moment. She was one of Dr. Cowan's three daughters. The room was available to rent and the Japanese man moved in. That visit would change Jessie's life forever.

The new guest was named Masataka Taketsuru. He was a member of a sake-distilling family in Japan. He had just finished a year of brewery training at home, but wanted to go on studying chemistry. He dreamed of distilling whisky one day. He attended the University of Glasgow to study organic and applied chemistry.

He wanted to do internships in some distilleries and he was invited by the Longmorn Distillery soon after. He was then able to undertake another internship at Hazelburn in Campbeltown.

Masataka and Rita.

In between, the Japanese man taught judo to one of Dr. Cowan's sons, but he continued to look at Jessie with admiration. Jessie noticed. Her father Samuel saw what was going on, but he was not very happy.

Masataka and Jessie married secretly in Glasgow on January 8, 1920. Dr. Cowan was furious when the couple finally confessed to him about the marriage. Jessie's mother Robina MacDonald didn't know what to think. In Japan, the Taketsuru family would be even more shocked by the news. Marrying for love was very uncommon in Japan.

Jessie secured a Japanese passport in September of the same year. Shortly afterwards, the couple travelled to Japan. They crossed the ocean to New York, travelled by train to Seattle, and boarded the Fushimi Maru, which would then take them to Yokohama and Kobe.

In Kobe, Jessie Cowan found a world where women had little say. Only the family could decide who could become husband and wife. Women owned nothing. They only 'lived' in their husband's houses. A woman walked behind her husband in the street, not next to him. Women were required to give their husbands heirs so that the line of the family could be continued. A man was permitted by society to knock on the door of another Japanese girl if his wife was not able to have children. But if a Japanese man was married to a foreign woman, that rule would not apply.

The Fushimi Maru.

By marrying a Scottish woman, Masataka (Jessie always called him Massan) had broken his family's line. Jessie had to rely on his total support at the beginning. He encouraged her to learn Japanese as soon as possible, which she did. She worked hard to master Japanese cooking, and she succeeded. But the couple quickly ran into financial concerns. To help, Jessie looked for a job. She was able to start as a teacher in English at the university thanks to British friends in Japan.

Masataka, in the meantime, worked at the beverage company Kotobukiya, which would later evolve into the beverage giant Suntory. He was involved in the construction of the first whisky distillery in Yamazaki. However, he dreamed of having his own distillery. A distillery just like those he had seen in Scotland. But perhaps on Hokkaido, the northern island that is very similar to Scotland in terms of landscape and climate.

In 1934, the couple finally moved north and settled in Yoichi.

HARD TIMES IN YOICHI

Masataka immediately started to realise his dream, the Yoichi Distillery. Jessie continued to work as an English teacher and gave piano lessons to help make ends meet. They then adopted a Japanese baby. But the project required a lot of money. Thanks to Jessie's financial

The beginning of Japanese whisky.

and moral support, Masataka was able to continue working on his plans. But money went out and little money came in. They had difficult years until 1940, when Masataka was able to produce his first 'Nikka' whisky.

When the Second World War broke out, Japan was at war with England. Many Japanese citizens disliked people from the west and those speaking English. Jessie was also looked at with renewed suspicion. Even her daughter Rima, now grown up, rebelled against her. After that, things never improved between them.

The Japanese government started taking actions against Jessie. She was visited by the police multiple times because she was suspected of espionage. But Jessie persevered. She used her colleagues at the university to find investors for the distillery. By the time she passed away in 1961, Nikka whisky had become a household name in Japan. And Jessie was considered 'a much-appreciated westerner'. The main street in Yoichi is still called 'Jessie Road'.

Masataka died in 1979. At the end of September 2014, the Japanese channel *NKH General* broadcast a drama series on TV in which the lives of Rita and Masataka were rolled out. The American actress, Charlotte Kate Fox played Rita. 149 episodes followed and the series became a huge success. The series also benefited the Yoichi Distillery. Sales increased by more than twenty percent that year and in 2014 the distillery received twice as many visitors as in the previous year.

QUIET PLEASE WHISKY SLEEPING

15

DAVID LLOYD GEORGE
THE MAN WHO CHANGED WHISKY FOREVER

The British history books describe David Lloyd George, who lived from 1863 to 1945, as a brilliant politician. He was from a poor family and became Prime Minister. However, he was much more than that. He served as both Minister for Commerce and Minister for Finance before the First World War. He was in charge of the munitions department in 1915, which became 'the Ministry of War' a year later.

Lloyd George made important innovations in the field of pensions and health insurance. He was on many occasions at odds with colleagues from his own party, often seen as the troublemaker.

He was not an Englishman but a Welsh native, a fact that received little attention in the history books. English was only his second language. His first language was Welsh.

Barrels at Ardbeg distillery.

David Lloyd George.

He was an incorrigible womanizer, a fact even less mentioned in the history books. His marriage fell apart because of this. He was also a teetotaler.

'Drink is doing more damage than all the German subs put together,' he shouted in Parliament in the spring of 1915. It was clear at that time that the war wouldn't be over by Christmas, as the government had communicated to the people. The frequent absences of workers in industry made things very difficult at a time when the demand for weapons was very high. Lloyd George believed that alcohol was to blame. His remedy was a complete ban on the production and sale of the 'demon drink'.

He announced it as such, but he hadn't counted on the response of the distillers. There were strong arguments against his proposal: the distillers produced alcohol not only for drinks, but also for the production of ammunition. They produced yeast as well. Yeast could no longer be imported from Belgium due to German blockades. No yeast, no bread. The minister was forced to peddle back, but he still made changes.

In May 1915, the Immature Spirits (Restriction) Act was published. It stated: 'No British or foreign spirits shall be delivered for home consumption unless they have been warehoused for a period of at least two years.'

BONDED WAREHOUSE

Whisky lovers can go to bed every night with peace of mind: They make a generous contribution to the treasury with every bottle of whisky purchased. Excise duties, apparently an invention of the Dutch, were introduced in Britain in the mid-seventeenth century, and the phenomenon, like all evil, quickly spread across the Continent. The VAT levy was added on top of the excise duties. VAT is not only calculated on the alcohol but on the excise duties as well (that means taxes on taxes).

The people had other concerns in 1915. The new spirit had to sit for years before it could be put into bottles. Fortunately, the idea of bonded warehouses had grown in the meantime: goods that required the payment of excise duties could be stored in a warehouse (locked up), with the aim of paying the excise duties when the goods were delivered. That made it more straightforward, but another problem arose: in which barrels should the drink be kept?

Initially, it was thought to use barrels in which sherry had been brought to England, en masse. The English were fond of sherry. Those barrels, once empty, remained in England anyway. Later, after Prohibition in America, the country was able to use an 'infinite' number of barrels of American oak. Most new whiskies in the US are put in a new barrel, so the old barrels were immediately put on sale.

Since then, a wide range of barrels has emerged from which whiskies draw the majority of their flavour. Remember that sixty to seventy percent of everything you find in your whisky is a gift from the barrel in which it was matured.

16

WAREHOUSE 6
THE SMALLEST IN THE WORLD?

Every distillery in Scotland has something that the others don't. Either it's the oldest, the youngest, the northernmost, or the highest. It goes on. Even if you don't get into the Guinness World Records book, it's important to stake a claim.

But there is something even better in Glenfarclas. They have 38 large maturing warehouses that can hold 105,000 barrels. The ripening warehouses are pretty similar. The gates are painted red with a heavy padlock and the walls are grey-black covered with an alcohol vapuor lusting fungus.

There is one warehouse that stands out at Glenfarclas: warehouse 6. You cannot miss it. You have to walk past it to get to the distillery. Warehouse 6 is hidden under a staircase that leads to a reception room. This warehouse is three metres wide, two metres deep, and one and a half metres high. There is a total of space for three barrels.

You don't get anything more in than that. This makes it officially the smallest HM Revenue & Customs accredited bonded warehouse in the UK. It's the smallest in the world, according to the Guinness World Records.

In 2013 one of the distillers whispered in the big boss's ear that it would be a good idea to draw more attention to the Glenfarclas. Why don't we make the smallest warehouse? Chairman John Grant was the first to be won over. One of the barrels in this special maturation warehouse is marked with the boss's signature.

The key question is: who owns the other two barrels? It remained a well-kept secret for a long time. But like all secrets, it was eventually revealed. True to the Glenfarclas tradition, all three barrels are sherry casks. John Grant's cask is a sherry butt filled in 2014. The sherry hogshead on the right, filled in 2011, belongs to His Royal Highness Prince Andrew, the Duke of York and the ex of the better-known redhead Sarah Ferguson.

The cask on the left is a sherry butt, filled in 1999 by none other than the legendary BBC weather forecaster and avid whisky enthusiast Ian McCaskill, who passed away in 2016. The witty way in which he kept reporting the weather made Britons believe that the UK had the best climate in the Northern Hemisphere. Proof that whisky makes everything better.

17

BAUDOINIA COMPNIACENSIS

THE WHISKY WORLD FULL OF MOULD

The strange sooty layer that covers the facades of the bonded warehouses and spreads merrily over every surface is something that anyone who has ever visited a distillery will know. We refer to it as a 'mushroom' or 'mould' but scientists speak of *Baudoinia compniacensis*, which actually means 'Baudoin from Cognac'.

Cognac?

Exactly.

The phenomenon does not only occur in whisky distilleries, but can be found in and around most places where alcohol vapours are present, anywhere in the world. Antonin Baudoin started to study the phenomena in the 1870s in the Cognac region. Hence, the name. The question was whether the fungus would be dangerous for human health or not. Much more thorough research, about a hundred years later, focused mainly on the whisky industry, which is why the fungus is most linked to whisky.

In Scotland, it's called the Distilleries' Shadow.

The fungus feeds on ethanol vapours. The carbon feed protects it against extreme temperature fluctuations. The fungus is able to tolerate low and high temperatures. And that is handy in a country like Scotland, where it is occasionally freezing, but where the sun can also hit hard (although that doesn't happen every day).

So it is these persistent ethanol guzzlers who consume the legendary 'angels' share' and not the angels themselves, as the Scots often tell us. Ethanol vapours are quite heavy and do not spread easily. The angels may be craving a mouthful of alcohol, but the vapours are unlikely to rise that high. That does not alter the fact that we can still find *Baudoinia compniacensis* hundreds of meters away from a distillery.

NOT EVERYONE'S FRIEND

According to scientists, *Baudoinia compniacensis* is harmless to humans, and for whisky enthusiasts, the fungus offers fantastic added value to the composition of their distillery pics. However, the fungus is not universally respected by those who live around or near the bonded warehouses. You can find the fungus not only on the walls, but also on plants, fences, garden furniture, and even on cars.

The hostility towards *Baudoinia* began in Kentucky, where savvy lawyers were able to claim substantial sums of money. It was expected that this practice might come to Scotland.

Diageo, the multinational producer of spirits and beer, is familiar with the story. They own a dozen 'secret' warehouses near Falkirk, Scotland, where whisky in hundreds of thousands of barrels was maturing. The local residents knew exactly where they were.

In 2012, some fifty families filed a complaint against Diageo. They demanded compensation. The action was progressed by a group of lawyers, but they achieved few results.

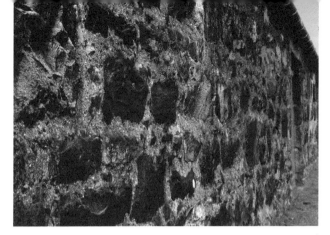

Chemical artworks.

In March 2017, Tom and Gail Chalmers, who live in Bonnybridge, about four hundred meters away from the warehouses, went to court. They demanded one hundred thousand pounds in damages from Diageo. Walls, rooves, terraces, garden furniture...everything was black. Even their daughter came back covered in black fungus after playing in the garden.

Diageo pointed out that the warehouses were already in place before the Chalmers arrived, so they should have been aware of the presence of whisky. What's more, according to Diageo (and also according to the Scotch Whisky Association), there was no proven link between *Baudoinia* and alcohol.

They tried by all means to have the complaint dismissed as inadmissible, knowing that – if the trial proceeded – they would face a total claim for damages of around a billion pounds.

The judge recently declared the complaint admissible.

The whole whisky world is waiting with trembling knees for the verdict.

18

SS POLITICIAN
A GIFT FROM THE GODS

In the early 1920s, six sister ships, ordered by Furness, Withy & Co of London, were launched at the shipyards of Furness, England, in Teesside. They were ultramodern and fast cargo ships for the time, intended to sail across all oceans. One of those ships, the *London Merchant*, served American ports on both the west and east coasts.

In 1935, after the great crisis, the Charente Steamship Company of Liverpool took over the *London Merchant*. They renamed the ship *SS Politician*. In 1939 the government requisitioned the ship for the connection between England, the United States, and the Caribbean. The *SS Politician* held out until the end of 1941, when it met its end. But it wasn't a German U-boat that sank the ship.

The Germans bombed the industrial zone between Edinburgh and Glasgow several times. The Secretary of State for Scotland, Tom Johnston, decided that the whisky stocks maturing in that area should be taken to safety as soon as possible.

The Sound of Eriskay.

SS Politician.

As a result, distillers and bottlers had huge quantities of whisky transferred to Liverpool so they could be shipped from there to America. The ship that was given the honour of delivering the first shipment was the *SS Politician*.

On February 3, 1940, at exactly 9:09 am in the morning, the *SS Politician* lifted the anchor and left the port of Liverpool in a light breeze and calm seas. Destination: Jamaica and New Orleans. The ship headed past the Isle of Man and then north. The route between the islands of the Hebrides was slightly safer. The lighthouses on the islands had been extinguished and painted black because of the war. So it became a 'blind' sailing. But those commanding the *SS Politician* believed that getting through wouldn't be a problem. All they needed was for the legendary Scottish weather to line up in the ships' favour.

But that turned out not to be the case. The next morning the weather quickly changed and once in the Sound of Eriskay, between Eriskay and South Uist, trouble really started: rough weather, lots of rocks, sandbanks, and the craziest ebb and flow.

At 7:40 am of February 5th, the *SS Politician* ran aground on a sandbank and immediately took in water. Twenty minutes later the engines gave up and the ship was at the mercy of the storm. No one on board knew exactly where they were. The rescue services didn't find the ship immediately because they had been given the wrong location. The residents of Uist and Eriskay knew better.

The SS Politician also carried a fortune in Jamaican money.

IN CASE OF EMERGENCY...

In addition to one thousand eight hundred bottles of stout and sherry, the *SS Politician* had a large load of whisky on board: 264,000 bottles: Ballantine's, Johnnie Walker, White Horse, Antiquary, and many other blends. The islanders were instantly ready to save as much of the contents of the bottles as they could. They still don't classify taking something from a stranded ship as 'theft', but as 'rescue'. The government sent a squad to locate the 'rescued' bottles.

A wave of checks and searches on the islands followed, with only part of the loot recovered. In September 1941 the wreck broke in half. The prow was pulled away to a demolition yard and the rest (containing some 12,000 more bottles) was blown up. In 1987, diver Donald MacPhee retrieved eight full bottles from the sea, two of which fetched more than £12,000 at an auction in 2013.

In 1947 the book *Whisky Galore*, a humorous account of this 'disaster', was written by Compton Mackenzie. Two years later, he co-wrote the script for the film of the same name with Angus MacPhail, remade in 2016. In 2009 a musical was also devoted to this incident.

But where are the rescued whiskies?

Nobody in the Hebrides knows.

19

AGOSTON HARASZTHY
BENEFICIARY OF THE SCOTTISH WHISKY INDUSTRY

Count Agoston Haraszthy was born in 1812 in Pest, Hungary. According to some sources, he was not a nobleman, although he liked to call himself an earl. In 1842, he called it quits in Hungary and left permanently for the United States. He settled with a family in Wisconsin, close to the city of Madison, on the Wisconsin River. He built a small town on the land he bought there.

Building was just one of his many abilities. He quickly manifested himself as a pig breeder, hop farmer, writer, steamboat operator, ferry manager, hunter, real estate agent, and even as a shepherd. All this did him no harm. But much of his money went to his great love, viticulture. He would produce Wisconsin wine.

He imported several grape varieties and established a model vineyard. The climate was not in his favour, and his business failed. He moved to California, where he settled in San Diego, but the climate in that area wasn't ideal for his grape growing plans either.

In 1856, he bought just 140 acres of land in Sonoma, about 60 miles north of San Francisco, to start a new vineyard. In 1857, he had Chinese 'guest workers' dig huge tunnels in a mountainside, intended as wine cellars. He bought more land until he owned about twenty square kilometres of vineyard: the Buena Vista Winery.

For a time, things went very well.

In fact, he was doing great.

The first brown spots appeared on his grapevines in 1860. Production came to a standstill as the plants slowly withered. The 'Count' did not know what the cause might be. Other vineyards in the region were affected as well.

Count Agoston Haraszthy.

'We may work too much with grape varieties from Eastern Europe,' he thought.

So in 1861 he travelled to Europe, passing through France, Switzerland, Germany, and Spain. He collected more than a hundred thousand cuttings from hundreds of grape varieties, which he took with him to the United States for new tests.

But he also left something behind in Europe. Without being aware. And the French were soon to experience it first-hand.

PHYLLOXERA VASTATRIX

The 'Count' was wrong about the brown spots on his grapevines.

They were not caused by the weather, or the origin of the grape, but by a creature no larger than a millimetre, with more legs than it needed, nasty feelers and – at a later stage – wings, twice as long as the beast itself: the grape louse, or *Phylloxera vastatrix*.

The Buena Vista Winery was heavily affected by the grape aphid.

Count Agoston Haraszthy was unaware that he had taken that little glutton to Europe, giving the animal and its millions of descendants the chance to gorge to their heart's content in Europe's vineyards. In 1870, more than seventy percent of French viticulture was ruined. Other wine countries were also affected.

One of the biggest victims was the cognac industry. Cognac soon became not only very expensive, but also very scarce. Unfortunately, Cognac was the favourite drink of the well-to-do Englishman, who purchased the drink in large quantities from France, and who was now running out.

The doors for Scottish whisky were suddenly wide open. By using Speyside-type whiskies, flavours could be created that suited the tastes of English ex-cognac drinkers. The whisky industry experienced a boom. The Scots owe much to 'Count' Agoston Haraszthy and his *Phylloxera vastatrix*.

20

WINSTON CHURCHILL

ALCOHOL OR NOT?

On December 12, 1899, during the Boer War in South Africa, a man named Winston Churchill, aged 25, escaped from a prisoner of war camp in Pretoria. He had been captured with British soldiers a month earlier. He was there as a reporter for the Morning Post and, being a journalist, was entitled to be released immediately. But the Boers believed he had fought (he had a weapon in his possession) and they would not let him go.

Churchill escaped through the toilets. The Boers immediately put a £25 bounty on his head. But he was already far away, riding on trains as a stowaway and eventually knocking on the door of a coalmine manager, who happened to be a Brit. The manager hid him in a mine shaft for three days and then put him on a train to Mozambique. Churchill immediately returned to South Africa and re-joined the British.

Ontsnapping uit Staatsmodelskool

Lasbrief vir joernalis Churchill uitgereik – en gekanselleer

Pretoria, 15 Desember – Die meeste van ons lesers is bewus daarvan dat Britse offisiere wat deur die Boeremagte krygsgevange geneem word, in die Staatsmodelskool in Pretoria aangehou word. Op Dinsdagnand, 12 Desember, het die enigste ontsnapping tot dusver uit die skoolterrein plaasgevind. Die gevangene wat weggekom het, is die joernalis Winston Churchill. Ons het verlede maand berig dat hy in Natal gevange geneem is toe die Boere 'n Britse gepantserde trein by Chievely oorrompel het. Joernaliste word normaalweg weer vrygelaat, maar Churchill het aktief aan die gevegg deelgeneem en het 'n rewolwer by hom gehad. Daarom is hy gevange geneem.

Nadat sy ontsnapping opgemerk is, is 'n lasbrief vir sy inhegtenisneming deur die owerheid uitgereik. 'n Paar uur later het 'n opdrag van kommandant-generaal Piet Joubert egter die oorlogskantoor in Pretoria per telegram bereik dat

Winston Churchill (REGS) as gevangene van die Transvaalse magte

Churchill as 'n burgerlike vrygelaat moet word. Die polisie-amptenare is gevolglik onmiddellik verwittig om die lasbrief vir sy inhegtenisname te ignoreer.

From the weekly magazine 'War Image'.

He was welcomed as a hero and his fame quickly spread to London. Winston Churchill was set up for a glorious career.

BUT WHERE WAS THE BOOZE?

It is rarely mentioned, but his heroic flight was totally unnecessary. The day after his escape, the Boers cancelled the bounty and the search was stopped. But what happened to his stock of liquor? When he left for South Africa, Churchill had brought with him a small stock: 38 bottles of wine, 18 bottles of whisky, and six bottles of brandy.

Enough to be seen as a 'boozer' for the rest of his life.

Is it true that Churchill depended on alcohol?

Churchill greets Blackie, the ship's mascot.

You won't find many photos of Churchill with a glass in his hand. That cannot be said of many of our politicians. On the other hand, you can easily find an image of him with a cigar. Or with the legendary 'V' sign, also sometimes with the palm turned towards himself (which quite obviously means something different than 'victory').

We know that, as a youngster, Churchill used to think whisky was 'disgusting'. It wasn't until he left for the battlefields of India and Afghanistan in the late 1800s that whisky came into his everyday life. He used it as a disinfectant for the dubious water they were given to drink. It would also become a part of his lifestyle: a small shot of whisky, generously supplemented with water. For the rest of his life, that mixture would be an indispensable part of his breakfast, alongside bacon and eggs. Johnnie Walker has a lot to thank him for.

And then there is that doctor's prescription.

On the evening of December 13, 1931, Winston Churchill was hit by a car on New York's Fifth Avenue. We can't find a clear description of his injuries anywhere, but we are sure that it was Dr. Otto C. Pickhardt who was instantly called in. From the doctor's certificate, we can deduce that Dr. Pickhardt made the correct diagnosis.

It was the middle of the American Prohibition, and alcohol was (in principle) only available for medical reasons. The doctor prescribed the following: '... for a speedy recovery of Mr. Churchill, a dose of distillates is necessary with meals. I recommend a daily dose

O.C. PICKHARDT, M.D.
117 EAST 80TH STREET
NEW YORK

January 26, 1932.

This is to certify that the post-accident conva-
lescence of the Hon. Winston S. Churchill necessitates
the use of alcoholic spirits especially at meal times.
The quantity is naturally indefinite but the minimum
requirements would be 250 cubic centimeters.

Signed:-

OCP:P   OTTO C. PICKHARDT, M.D.

Doctor's note, probably a forgery.

of at least 25 centilitres.' The certificate still exists, but has been labelled as 'false' by several researchers.

Indeed, many historians exonerate Winston Churchill from 'dependence on the bottle'. To support their theory, they cite some of his quotes, confirming that he hated people who could not live without alcohol.

But on the other hand, a bill was introduced in the United Kingdom in 1942 to close all distilleries and use the grains only for bread. But Churchill made sure that nothing came of it.

21

ARCHIBALD HADDOCK

NO MORE ALCOHOL FOR HIM

At the beginning of the last century, a British seaman named Archibald Haddock was born. An exact date is not available. We do not have much information about his past either. We know that he was a descendant of Sir Francis Haddock, who went to the ocean, in the 17th century, in the service of the English King Charles II. Had it not been for the fact that Georges Remi, better known all over the world as Hergé, introduced Archibald Haddock to us in 1941, he would have remained a total stranger.

Fortunately, we were introduced to Archibald's ultimate vocabulary of swearing, his unique talent for fulmination, his flexibility in devising curses, and his sacred affinity for whisky.

In 1958, the publisher wanted to bring the Tintin volume 'The Crab with the Golden Claws' to the United States. They would be permitted only if there were no alcohol references or alcohol jokes. America takes care of the souls of its citizens.

The story of that volume is about a bully and incorrigible drunk named Haddock, who makes his first appearance and drinks throughout the whole story. Do we, Europeans, give such books to our children for "relaxation"? Yes, we do. Exemplary parents!

Do you really think Haddock is the only character who is occasionally 'a little tipsy'? Forget it. Open the books. Pay special attention to that 'sweet' rough-haired fox terrier, Snowy. You can hardly call that dog a teetotaler either. And Tintin himself? An example for the youth? Come on, you make me laugh!

Take 'Tintin in Tibet'. This is where Haddock goes completely over the line: he is carrying a backpack full of booze. Even worse: at the first slump during the trip, he drinks a whole bottle and becomes instantly 'exhausted'. Too bad. But wait: not even three pages after that, it's Snowy's turn. Apparently, there was a broken bottle in the captain's backpack and Snowy was all too aware. The dog knew how to catch every drop, until he too became completely insane, stumbling into the depths (on the last picture of that page, of course). Imagine: you don't even know if the animal will live or die. (Spoiler: Snowy survives.)

TINTIN... NO!

When you thought this was the worst thing that could happen, you were wrong. Only fifteen pages after that, Tintin (yes, you read that right: TINTIN) pulls a bottle of brandy from his backpack. Cognac! Did we not hear him say somewhere that he never drank alcohol? Absolutely, more than once. Liar. I can submit pictures of him with too much wine and champagne.

But wait. It gets even worse. In 'The Red Sea Sharks', on page 22, it turns out that Tintin always has a bottle of rum in his pocket. Rum! 'I always have it with me for emergencies,' he says. Typical subterfuge of people who drink. Look at 'The Broken Ear'. There he pours aguardiente as if it was water. No wonder he doesn't remember having to face the firing squad on the next page. If you don't learn from that, then I don't know what to teach you.

And all this 'for the youth from 7 to 77 years', as the Tintin magazine always proclaimed.

Fortunately, there is still Professor Calculus.

In 'Tintin and the Picaros', Hergé's latest album, Calculus bravely puts an end to a Sodom-and-Gomorrah-like festival. The so often absent-minded professor uses several medicinal plants to develop odourless and tasteless tablets. Whoever takes even one of these tablets will never again imbibe a drop of alcohol.

Ingenious.

Did Calculus ever receive the Nobel Prize for this? Never. That says enough about the Nobel Prize.

Let's all raise a glass to Professor Calculus, to Captain Haddock, Tintin and Snowy, and to Hergé's endless talent.

P.S. Captain Haddock also took one of Professor Calculus' pills. So, from now on he walks casually past every whisky bottle. Without looking back. Oof.

22

"WEEL DONE CUTTY SARK"

WHISKY AND WITCHES

Cutty Sark whisky was intended for the American market (and Americans love it), but you will know the bottle: an ordinary straight bottle with a large canary-yellow label (the glowing yellow was actually a misprint of the first printer). It shows a drawing of a three-master. Underneath, in handwritten letters are the words 'Cutty Sark'. The initial label mentioned that the whisky was 'Scots'. This bewildered the Scots, because whisky from Scotland is normally called 'Scotch'. Since then, the label has been adjusted.

The Cutty Sark blend was created around 1923, at the beginning of American Prohibition. At that time in the US, whisky was no longer allowed to be distilled or sold. But the sale of illegal whisky was in full swing. A lot of whiskies, imported from Europe, came to the United States via the Bahamas.

Francis Berry, working for the London liquor merchants Berry Brothers & Rutt, travelled to Nassau in the Bahamas in 1921 and whilst there (reputedly) met the legendary Captain McCoy. McCoy was the most notorious smuggler in the US, the man behind the equally legendary 'Real McCoy' whisky.

Francis Berry came back home with a few new ideas: "The Americans want a light-coloured whisky; light and fruity!" he declared.

Berry Brothers & Rutt had no problems in creating that new whisky. They already had a market for it: the US. There was only one thing that was missing: a strong name. During a meeting, James McBey, the designer of the label, came up with something very unusual: Cutty Sark. There was a moment of silent reflection. But some knew right away where he got the name.

THE CLIPPER CUTTY SARK

A three-master training ship had been in service at Falmouth, Cornwall, since 1922. It was a fairly well-known clipper: Cutty Sark, built in 1869 on the Dunbarton yards in Scotland. It was one of the last, but also one of the fastest tea ships ever built. The Cutty Sark made eight voyages from London to China to pick up tea. In 1871 the ship needed only 107 days for this trip; a record.

But sailing ships fell into oblivion after steamships became popular and because the Suez-canal shortened the route to the East.

So the Cutty Sark vessel found a new purpose. From 1873 the ship connected England with Australia for the transport of wool. A Portuguese shipowner bought the clipper twelve years later and renamed her 'Ferreira'. The clipper fell into a state of disrepair thereafter.

Thanks to a retired British sea captain, it would eventually land in Cornwall and regain its old name.

The ship has been in the Greenwich Maritime Museum since 1954. After fires in 2007 and 2014, it was completely restored and can now be visited. Pay special attention to the figurehead: a very scantily dressed, busty lady who is holding a ponytail. This lady is Nannie the Witch.

TAM O'SHANTER

Robert Burns, a fervent womaniser, alcohol lover, temporary excise inspector, but best known as Scotland's national poet, penned a long, pedantic poem in 1790 in which Tam o'Shanter plays the leading role. Tam is a farmer who regularly goes to the pub with his faithful mare Meg. One night he drives back home 'fully loaded' and sees that a party is taking place in the local church: a band of witches dance and jump around as the devil plays the bagpipes. Tam discovers that the witches reveal themselves more and more with each new song.

By the end, Tam had seen the half-naked Nannie. She was wearing a shirt that was way too short, a 'cutty sark' in Scottish. Tam couldn't hold it together any longer. He yelled out, "Weel done, Cutty-sark."

The witches notice him and attack. Knowing that witches can't cross rivers, he urges Meg to run to the River Doon. Just as Meg dives into the water, Nannie grips Meg's tail and cuts it.

But Tam is saved.

We'll end with good advice (and with the last lines from Tam o'Shanter):

> Now, who this tale of truth shall read,
> Each man, and mother's son, take heed:
> Whenever to drink you are inclined,
>
> Or short skirts run into your mind,
> Think! you may buy joys over dear:
> Remember Tam o' Shanter's mare.

In 1897 Henry Sturmey, editor-in-chief of The Autocar Magazine, decided to drive a Daimler (the eighth Daimler ever built) from John O'Groats, in the northeast of Scotland, to Land's End in southwestern Cornwall. No one had ever done that before. Many in the UK felt that this was a dangerous and virtually impossible enterprise.

But Sturmey did it. He was even able to do it with an average speed of almost twelve kilometres per hour. Ten years earlier, a correspondent for *Harper's Weekly Gazette* suddenly put forward a completely different idea: he wanted to visit all the distilleries in Scotland, Ireland, and England. He could not make use of a "luxury" Daimler and would hence have to content himself with train (first class, actually), carriage, horse, and pony.

Fortunately, the rail network was already extensively developed in the UK.

Let's have a look at page 505 in Baedekers 'Great Britain. Handbook for Travelers' published in 1890. 'From Inverness to Thurso and Wick', there were two connections a day. The

Alfred Barnard.

journey cost 26 shillings and took six to eight hours depending on the weather. That's not bad, knowing that the distance is 170 kilometres.

The man behind this amazing whisky tour idea was an energetic guy, born around 1837 in Thaxted, England: Alfred Barnard. His father was a grocer.

We know little about his rather bumpy career. We find him here and there as a 'soap seller' and a 'trader'. Later, he came up with a private advertising agency that advertised groceries, wines, and drinks. Maybe the switch from the advertising world to *Harper's Weekly Gazette* in London was for Barnard but a small step. He began his tour in 1885 and it would take almost two years to visit and describe the 162 distilleries in his book. Most of it was taken up by Scottish distilleries, 129 in total. Ireland had only 29 included and just four were found in England.

It was a good time for the Scottish distilleries: the blended whiskies arrived in the market around 1860 and those blended whiskies were an immediate success. The distilleries in Scotland were doing very well. That was not the case for their Irish colleagues. In Ireland, the whisky industry was in big trouble.

UNIQUE DOCUMENT

Barnard describes each visit with great attention to detail. None of the facts escaped his pen. There is was a cheerful tone where it was appropriate and a serious tone where needed.

Sometimes he paid more attention to the road on which the distillery was located or to the nature around it, than to the business itself. But the tour was a good school for him to learn about whisky. He goes further into the production process as the book progresses. He says more, for example, about the shape of the stills.

Cragganmore Distillery.

He may have been a novice at the beginning of the journey, but his work offers a unique picture of the entire whisky industry in the 19th century.

Several of the distilleries described have already vanished, but in this way, reading about the others is more compelling. They are especially of interest to those who already visited those distilleries today.

Anyone who has driven on Islay from Port Ellen to Bowmore will recognise Barnard's description:

'We found the coach drive from Port Ellen to Bowmore one of the most uninteresting that we had ever experienced. During the journey of four hours, we saw two or three habitations, and scarcely any trees; in all our wanderings, we have never travelled by such a dismal and lonely road. Fortunately, we were in a large party and a merry one, or we should have wearied of the dismal track long before we reached our destination. Sandy, our aged coachman, was a character, and drove us at about the rate of four miles an hour... We plied him with nips of whisky to urge his steeds along, but no persuasions would induce him to trot his horses... Some of us walked many a mile, and were yet able to keep ahead of him.''

It has not changed very much on Islay.

24

THE QUAICH

CUP OF FRIENDSHIP

The quaich (pronounced 'kweich') is a low, round saucer, most often wide and shallow, with two horizontal handles. It is named after the Gaelic 'cuach', which means 'little bowl'. They can be found in all sizes and they are usually very well crafted.

Today, the role of the quaichs is mostly ceremonial, but they used to be the preferred cup for drinking whisky. In the Middle Ages, scallops were used as a drinking bowl. Some consider the scallop to be the model on which the development of the quaich was based.

The quaich is referenced in documents as early as the 17th century, demonstrating that it was in full use throughout Scotland at the time. There are quaichs in silver and gold, but often also in pewter, wood, horn, or bone. Similar to barrels, they were made initially from wooden staves. This required a great deal of craftsmanship. The copies that are left are now preserved as art objects.

The Keepers' legendary Quaich.

The silversmiths came onto the market with their copies in the second half of the 17th century. Originally, the lines of the wooden staves were mimicked in the metal. The decorations applied to the quaichs—to the two handles, on the outer wall of the bowl, and in the bottom of the quaich—are the real art value of such antique specimens. Craftsmen often made use of Celtic knot drawings, leaf drawings, and stylized cornstalks. In the bottom we usually find the coat of arms of the owner.

ALWAYS WATCH OUT

The two handles have a very important function: you can use them even if it becomes more difficult to keep the cup horizontal after several drams. In the first place, the idea is to hold the nicely filled cup with one hand and give it to a visitor who can immediately grab the other handle and drink. When a group of people have to take a sip, it means the quaich can go around easily. For this reason, the quaich is known as 'the cup of friendship'.

Every self-respecting whisky drinker had their own personal quaich, carrying it with them in case of emergencies. The quaichs of known historical figures are cherished in museums.

The quaich slowly fell into oblivion in the last century. It lost its status as a 'drinking cup', but eventually gained significance as a festive symbol. It features in many museums as a window into historical fact.

Sir Walter Scott, a collector of quaichs, owned the legendary *Waterloo Quaich*, which was made in London in 1824 of silver and elm wood.

He brought the elm wood back with him from the battlefield of Waterloo. He took it from a tree growing on the field when he visited the place. It wasn't just any elm tree, but the elm tree under which the Duke of Wellington had stood when he had given orders to his troops in 1815. The same elm had been visited by many people.

Sir Walter Scott.

This quaich was stolen from Abbodsford, where Scott lived, in 1999. Fourteen years later, it was found in a French antique shop.

Fittingly, that *Waterloo Quaich* carries a motto.

The motto reads: "Always look out."

25

THE PATTISON BROTHERS

WHISKY AND PARROTS

The Pattison family started a successful dairy wholesaler in Edinburgh in 1847. Robert and Walter Pattison took over the business in the late 19th century as the second generation.

Together with Alexander Elder, they relaunched their company under the name Pattison, Elder & Co.

They would go on to receive a lot of attention and to make headlines.

Even though they could live well as a dairy wholesaler, the brothers realised that the big profits were somewhere else: whisky. They started blending whisky in 1887. It was a good moment to start: the phylloxera, the grape louse, struck in France. The British ran out of supplies of brandy and very quickly switched to buying blended whisky.

Pattisons WHISKY

"Victorious all along the line"

THE BOOMING OF THE CANNON

is nothing to the "booming" of Pattisons' Whisky. Steady, unaltering attention to the object aimed at hits the mark and wins the battle. Pattisons' have aimed at hitting the public taste for a pure, sound, fully-matured, delicately-flavoured whisky, and they have succeeded. Pattisons' Whisky is the Scotch spirit in its perfection—wholesome, stimulating, and cream-like. Pattisons' Whisky has fought its way to the front and will remain there.

Sole Proprietors:
PATTISONS, LTD., Highland Distillers, BALLINDALLOCH, LEITH, & LONDON.
Head Offices: CONSTITUTION STREET, LEITH.

BIG BOOM

Pattisons Ltd. spent huge amounts of money on advertising.

At the time, blended whisky was a fairly new product, but it became fashionable as the product of the day. It turned out that there were huge profits awaiting the Pattisons.

By 1889, their small company had already made a profit of more than one hundred thousand pounds. The following years were even more profitable. In 1892 they decided not just to blend someone else's whisky, but to distil whisky themselves. The company floated on the stock exchange and its name was changed to Pattisons Ltd.

Pattisons Ltd. bought half the shares of Glenfarclas, and it also acquired interests in Oban, Aultmore, and the Ardgowan Grain Distillery. The Pattison brothers were successful and they loved showing it to the outside world.

They spent huge sums on advertising: in 1897 they spent an advertising budget of over £60,000 UK pounds in the UK alone, the equivalent of which would be about five million in today's money.

But they didn't make it out of advertising alone. They also trained fifty African grey parrots to shout two phrases continuously: 'Pattisons' Whisky is best' and 'Buy Pattisons' Whisky'. They gifted these animals, in gilded cages, to liquor stores in Liverpool. According to other sources, it might have been five hundred parrots. Pattisons linked a newspaper campaign to the parrot initiative with the slogan 'Pattisons' whisky? It speaks for itself'.

But the success of the Pattisons was largely reliant on borrowed money, manipulated balance sheets, and other clever tricks: stocks were sold at high prices and quietly bought back at a lower cost; bills of exchange were discounted before maturity; on paper, stocks were overstated, and the dividends were paid to shareholders with borrowed money to save appearances.

In addition to that, it was discovered that the Pattisons were not very accurate with what they wrote on the labels of their bottles. For example, they mixed very cheap grain alcohol with a small amount of malt whisky, and labelled the bottle as 'Fine Old Glenlivet', for sale at a good price. More people became suspicious of the situation. The first bank to decline to pay a Pattison check was the Clydesdale Bank.

News spread quickly that the Pattisons were in discussion with the banks. Alarm bells sounded throughout the whisky world.

The stock market value of the Pattinsons' shares crashed catastrophically on December 5, 1898. They diminished by 55 percent in one fell swoop. The group of creditors was so large that a whole swathe of distilleries and blenders, old and new, were also brought down with Pattisons Ltd.

Many companies went out of business. Several people had followed the brothers' enthusiasm and, as a result, a huge stock of whisky had been created for which there was no immediate demand.

The price of whisky dropped like a lead balloon.

On April 8, 1901, Robert and Walter Pattison were arrested, only to be released on bail a few days later. Their trial started two months later, the case lasting nine days. Robert was sentenced to eighteen months in prison, Walter to eight months.

But 'one man's misfortune is another man's opportunity'. The 'Pattison Crash' would be particularly good news for someone else. The Distillers Company (DCL), which would eventually become Diageo, bought the entire Pattison stock, along with a number of the distilleries that were closed down.

The price that Diageo paid was so low, it was ridiculous.

26

FATHER MATHEW
WHISKEY HATER, WHISKEY KILLER

Father Theobald Mathew was born in 1790 and came from a poor Irish family. He joined the Capuchin Order when he was eighteen. He became a priest six years later. The man was primarily committed to helping the poor of the nineteenth century. When he was 24 years old, Theobald Mathew started a crusade against all that was excess and uninhibitedness.

Life was hard for many Irish people then. Cholera struck. Hunger was never far away. Many people took refuge in alcohol. The government's attempts to curb this were unsuccessful.

Father Mathew started his 'Total Abstinence Movement' on April 10, 1838. He called for everyone to switch to total abstinence during a public meeting on that day. He was the first to solemnly vow never to touch alcohol again for the rest of his life. The sixty audience members made the same vow that night.

Father Mathew's group of followers grew continuously as meetings followed one after the other. After three months, 25,000 people in Cork had taken the oath. The number of followers increased to 130,000 within two months. Father Mathew travelled across the country and the list of followers grew by the thousands every day. He gained 70 thousand new members in a single day in Dublin.

At the height of his movement, more than three million Irishmen had taken the oath. That was more than half of the Irish adult population. Children took the oath as well and some still do today.

In all the towns of Ireland and England, Temperance Halls were erected and furnished and hosted regular lectures to convince even more people to join the group.

Father Mathew preached in the US for two years, starting in 1849. Hundreds of thousands of Americans followed him in his 'Total Abstinence Movement'. But he made a big mistake. The anti-slavery movement was greatly expanding in the US at that time and he chose the side of those who wanted to preserve slavery. 'In the Bible, slavery was never marked as not done!' he once said.

It was necessary for him to return to Ireland early. He continued his moralising journey in his homeland. But the costs of these activities were high. Soon, he was no longer able to pay his debts. He was arrested and sent to prison. He died five years later, in 1856, and was buried in Cork, where a statue was erected in his honour.

There were over 20,000 pubs in Ireland when Father Mathew started his campaign. In the space of six years, the number fell to 13,000. But it was more than just the drinking establishments that went bankrupt. Many distilleries were forced to close as well, because they didn't enjoy enough sales to stay open.

But Father Mathew should not be blamed for everything.

The Irish whiskey industry has taken a lot of blows: beginning with World War I, and followed by the Irish War of Independence, from 1916 to 1921. As a result of independence, the whole British Empire immediately vanished as a market for the 'Irish Free State'.

And exactly when the Irish were starting to concentrate on the American market, Prohibition, which would last until after 1933, prevented the sale of alcohol.

World War II broke out seven years after that. Grains were no longer allowed to be used for whiskey. The final blow to the Irish whiskey market came at the end of that war. American liberators had a clear preference for Scotch whiskey and spread scotch all over Ireland (in addition to chewing gum and nylon stockings).

When the 'sixties' arrived, only five Irish distilleries remained. Two hundred years previously, there had been about two thousand. Even the pubs disappeared. There were almost no pubs left.

After 1960, the remaining distilleries started working together to put the proud Irish whiskey back on the world market.

Since then, whiskey has been written with an 'e' in Ireland.

And now, look at the map: more than thirty distilleries today. The (whiskey) world is changing fast.

W B Todd

27

ROBERT BENTLEY TODD

'FATHER' OF THE HOT TODDY

Do you feel a bit sick? Make a note of the following recipe, which will help you feel better: put a large dash of whisky (by 'large' I mean really 'large') in a mug or glass, add a small amount of water (by 'small' I really mean 'small'), then take a lemon and squeeze it in. Next, add some tea and herbs. I'm thinking of thyme, sage, cinnamon, cloves, and whatever else comes to your mind. Add some fruit: apple, pear, banana if necessary. And finally, a spoonful of honey.

To finish, heat the whole thing up in a microwave. It is very simple after that: you drink this delicious mixture, you run to your bed, you cover yourself warmly, and you sleep like a marmot all night long.

You can run a marathon the next day.

🍸 The famous 'Hot Toddy'.

The recipe is not mine. It can be found everywhere as 'Hot Toddy'.

Some troublemakers claim that the name Toddy is derived from an Asian drink, while Irishmen (who always know better) insist it was named after the Irish doctor Robert Bentley Todd. It is not likely that he came up with the recipe himself, but his methods suggest that this might have been possible.

Doctors like certain expressions.

'Less' or 'none' are their favourite words when combined with tasty things. 'More' or 'a lot' are words they prefer for things less tasty. But Doctor Robert Todd looked at things a different way.

Robert Todd, born in 1809, son of a well-known doctor, never considered becoming a doctor at the beginning, but moved in that direction after his father's death. He would become famous himself, not only as a sought-after speaker, but for his well-considered theories. He focused on physiological medicine, brand new at the time. He specialised in medicine related to fever and in particular, delirium tremens. He was certain that drugs being prescribed at that time would do nothing to heal the patient.

The healing needed to come from inside, according to Todd. Best of all, with alcohol. After all, according to him, the body could fight every disease by converting alcohol into vitamins.

Accordingly, the best therapy was always to administer alcohol. The healing process could take a lot of time. Therefore, it was important to hope that the patient would live long enough until he was cured. That was the only weakness in his theory: it did not always work.

Years later scientists were able to confirm that the body does not convert alcohol into nutritious elements. This news came a little too late for Charles Hindley, a Member of Parliament. In 1857, he had symptoms of delirium and suffered from hallucinations. His primary care physician, Dr. Granville, treated him with reasonable success through bloodletting and mustard baths. However, according to the patient's family, this was not going fast enough. Without the knowledge of Doctor Granville, Todd was called in for help. He made a quick diagnosis and immediately devised the necessary treatment: five centilitres of cognac every half hour (the English were still in their 'cognac period' at the time).

After a single day, the patient complained much less, but he was not as awake as before. This 'success' prompted Todd to double the dose.

Charles Hindley died two days later after drinking more than three litres of brandy. Dr. Granville understood what had happened but was so collegiate as to report 'cardiac arrest' as the cause of death on the death certificate.

And then on January 30, 1860, Dr. Robert Bentley Todd died from an overdose of the same drug.

Still Life with BOTTLE

500 YEARS OLD

Established 1494
Single Malt Scotch Whisky
GLEN
BOTTLEGON
100% vol. 70cl

28

RALPH STEADMAN
STILL LIFE WITH BOTTLE

The Western world has seen more new whisky books in the past fifty years than in the previous five centuries. Many of those books are very similar. Yet there is one that stands out above all the others and which should not be missing in your whisky library: a book by Ralph Steadman.

Steadman was born in Chester in 1936 and grew up in Wales. He juggles words and lines, and he throws colours as an artist. His works of art can be found in many museums, in magazines such as *Punch*, in newspapers such as *The Daily Telegraph* and *The New York Times*, in wonderful adaptations of literary gems such as *Alice in Wonderland* and *Animal Farm*, on record covers of Zappa and The Who (among others), on labels for beer and wine, in children's books, on posters, etc. He often provides the illustrations as well as the cheerful content for other types of books, like books about Leonardo da Vinci or French wine.

He also provided the illustrations for a masterpiece about whisky: 'Still Life with Bottle'. The subtitle is: 'Whisky according to Ralph Steadman'.

The author travelled for a long time through Scotland and its islands to create that book. He chatted with natives over a dram, jotted down their 'wisdoms', and artfully mixed them with his own ingenuity. Ralph Steadman skillfully played the Englishman out against the Scot, summarising battles in a few words and recapitulating Scottish history as if it was a tasting note.

The history of distilling is well documented in his work of course, although he occasionally gives it his own funny twist. He visited distilleries, cooperages, castles and pubs, and even gives a colourful account of his experiences at Blair Castle, at the Keepers of the Quaich's dinner.

In his work, you will meet legendary and less legendary Scots and you will learn the tricks of the trade: from malting to smuggling. But above everything, you are absorbed by his masterful illustrations.

Ralph Steadman is best known for his collaboration with the American journalist Hunter Thompson, author of 'Fear and Loathing in Las Vegas', among others. The Americans were fonder of Steadman's work than the British.

Abroad, several beverage manufacturers asked Steadman to design their labels: Montes in Chile, Bonny Doon Vineyard in California, and Kaesler Wines in Australia, for instance.

But Steadman got the most attention with his designs for the Flying Dog Brewery in Maryland. This small craft brewery requested him to design a label for one of their first beers. They didn't have a name yet. He promised to find one, based on what he had heard during the brainstorming at the brewery.

He created a beautiful label, with the slogan 'Good Beer No Shit'. They accepted the design. But when the beer hit the market, it turned out that not everyone could live with this little work of art. There was an obscenity complaint filed, and the bottles had to be removed from the shelves. The slogan was temporarily changed to 'Good Beer No Censorship'. In 2001, a judge in California ruled that Flying Dog had not committed an offense. Flying Dog continued to work with Steadman and launched new labels such as 'Raging Bitch Belgian-Style IPA' (made with Belgian yeast) and 'Easy IPA', which was given a playful character that looked like it had just been plucked from a children's story.

Strathisla Distillery.

The latter didn't do very well, especially in the UK, as it was felt that children might think it was a soft drink. 'It's an encouragement to drink,' they said. The most significant opposition to Flying Dog and Steadman came with the release of the Cardinal 'Spiced' Zin wine. The image of the cardinal on the label didn't look very Catholic or peace-loving. On the contrary, it appeared rather terrifying. They had a lot of trouble with it in Ohio and other states.

But Steadman continues to draw, paint, write, and compose in his very own style. He refuses to sell any of his original works.

'If anyone owns a Steadman original, it's stolen,' he says.

(*Still Life with Bottle* is published by Ebury Press in London)

29

CHARLES II OF NAVARRE

AQUA VITAE AS A LAST REMEDY

Charles II of Navarre rarely gets much space in the history books. His nicknames were 'Charles the Bad' or 'Charles the Evil One'.

In the middle of the fourteenth century (1332-1387), Navarre was a small kingdom in the north of Spain, close to the Pyrenees, but also linked in a crazy way to France. Charles II was in fact the son of Philip of Evreux and Joan of Navarre, but – more importantly – he was also the grandson of Louis X of France.

Charles II might have made a claim to the French throne. But that didn't happen. During the Hundred Years War, he hooked up with the English against France and ended up in prison. He also fought some battles in Spain after that, with too little success to make the front pages.

Charles II.

At the end of his life, Charles II suffered diabolical pains in his limbs. He was barely able to move his arms or legs. Doctors in the fourteenth century had a remedy: aqua vitae, or whisky.

But it wasn't to drink. It was to apply through the skin. The doctors said that Charles II should be wrapped every night in linen cloths which were imbued with aqua vitae. It was believed that this would relax the muscles, loosen the joints, and relieve the pain. And it helped.

Until that very last night. The maid wrapped the fabrics around Charles and sewed them together with large stitches. Instead of cutting the last thread with scissors as usual, she burned it with a candle.

We know a lot of kings had warm feelings for their maidens, but there are very few maids who set their king ablaze.

LAGGANMORE DISTILLERY

ROMANTIC, FAKE WHISKY

One of Britain's most watched TV series was 'Monarch of The Glen' on BBC ONE, between 2000 and 2005. The series was named after Sir Edwin Landseer's famous painting (mentioned elsewhere in this book).

In the 64 episodes of the series, we learn the story of a London restaurateur who, after the death of his father, inherits a slightly dilapidated mansion in the Highlands. He doubts whether he should take it over, but finally decides to take a chance and to breathe new life into Glenbogle.

The series enjoyed seven seasons. The majority of shooting for the series took place in the vicinity of Grantown-on-Spey, with Speyside and the Cairngorms as the backdrop.

Some ingredients of the series: love, fidelity, infidelity, triangle and quadrilateral relationships, legal, illegitimate, and concealed children, financial successes and failures, maids coming and maids going, marriages and divorces, handsome dance teachers and ghosts.

And last, but not least: a real whisky distillery: Lagganmore Distillery.

Those who are looking for the town of Lagganmore will be disappointed. It's not on the map. The only Lagganmore I found was a bus stop on the Main Street in the harbour town of Stranraer, on the west coast of Dumfries and Galloway.

Laggan does exist as a village on the Spey, west of Newtonmore. And there is a Loch Laggan near the Dalwhinnie Distillery. And there's also a Lagganmore Hotel and Golf Club (but check first to see if it is still open).

And then there was the Battle of Lagganmore in 1664. This brawl near Loch Scammadale must have been quite meaningless, as there are few historical references. It was a tussle between the eternal enemies Clan MacDonald and Clan Campbell. The Clan MacDonald won.

At Loch Scammadale, however, you will not find a distillery.

Nevertheless, a lot of Lagganmore whisky is served in Monarch of The Glenn.

Just like the many passages of love and hate in the series, the brand of the whisky in the series was fake too.

But it really was whisky: the distillery scenes were shot at Speyside Distillery, in the beautiful countryside around Drumguish.

In the bottles was a delicious Speyside whisky, twelve years old.

CERTIFICATE

The largest spirit tasting was
achieved by 2,252 participants
in an event organised by
Whisky Unlimited in
Gent, Belgium,
on 31 January 2009

GUINNESS WORLD RECORDS LTD

31

WHISKY AND RECORDS

THE MORE THE BETTER

Hearing about whisky records, one thinks of the huge sums a wealthy sheik might be willing to pay for an ordinary, if rare, bottle of whisky that he or she – no matter how crazy they are – will probably never taste.

At the end of February 2020, a bottle of The Macallan 1926, labelled by artist Valerio Adami, was sold at the Whisky Auctioneer (in Perthshire) for a whopping US$1,072,000. It was the highest amount ever paid online for a bottle of whisky. Bids were made from eleven different countries, including Australia and Singapore. The bottle eventually remained in Europe.

Everyone who follows whisky knows that this record will be broken again. But there is a very different whisky record which some believe can be broken. Until today, all attempts have been unsuccessful.

On January 31, 2009 (an icy cold day, at minus seven degrees Celsius), the organisers of the International Malt Whisky Festival in Ghent (Wouter Wapenaar and myself), in collaboration

Joining us to beat those Swedes.

with the Flemish Caledonian Society, brought together no less than 2,252 whisky lovers to taste collectively six different whiskies. We received the support of whisky drinkers from Wallonia, Northern France, and the Netherlands.

All 2,252 tasters received a tray with six small bottles, provided by Diageo.

Due to the winter cold, we suspected some participants of having grabbed the bottles a little too early. In any case, the adjudicator of the record attempt was standing by and did not join in the drink, but carefully counted all those present and watched them taste the whiskies together.

With 2,252 participants, we smashed the record of the Swedes from 2001, where a bunch of enthusiasts in Stockholm brought together 1,221 tasters (serving only five whiskies and not six).

Our record attempt was attended by Swedish newspaper and TV journalists. They stayed two days longer than planned and, in the end, resigned themselves to defeat. You know about those Swedes. As Ikea says: "The Swedes are not that crazy."

Those Swedish drinkers tried again to sink our record once more after that. Of course, it was in vain.

32

CARRY AMELIA MOORE

"ALL NATIONS WELCOME, BUT CARRY!"

Carry Amelia Moore was born in Kentucky in 1846. Her name was actually Carrie, but she used both versions. Carry had Scottish roots: her mother Mary was a Campbell, her father George, an Irishman. She married twice, first to Missouri doctor Charles Gloyd who was an alcoholic. He would die two years after the marriage, but in the meantime, they were already divorced.

Eight years later Carry married again, this time to David Nation: a preacher, lawyer, and journalist. The couple moved to Texas. Carry was in charge. She even wrote his sermons. If he went on for too long during his sermons, she just yelled that enough was enough. The family

DEDICATED TO THE WOMENS CRUSADE
Against Liquor Throughout the World

TEMPERANCE

SONG AND CHORUS

THE LIPS
THAT TOUCH
LIQUOR
SHALL NEVER
TOUCH MINE

WORDS BY SAM BOOTH.

MUSIC BY GEO. T. EVANS.

Price 40 Cts.

M. Gray
PUBLISHER

623 & 625 CLAY ST.
SAN FRANCISCO.

101 FIRST STREET
PORTLAND, O.

regularly had problems and was sometimes forced to move, eventually ending up in Kansas. Carry and David divorced in 1901.

But it all worked out pretty well for Carry. From her second husband she borrowed the name Nation, cleverly combining it with her first name so that she became known as 'Carry A. Nation'. It would also become her slogan: the nation could count on her.

Around 1899 Carry received, as she called it, a 'divine message'. She was called to tackle the drinking problem in the United States. Getting such 'divine' messages ran in the family. For example, her mother had believed for several years that she was a lady-in-waiting to Queen Victoria.

Later, Carry's mother developed that idea further: she was convinced that she was Victoria herself. She ended up in an institution. Two of Carry's sisters went down a similar path.

The authoritarian Carry A. Nation.

Carry took action in a subdued manner first: she started to sing battle songs against alcohol in saloons, immediately gaining followers. Later, to make an even bigger impression, she smashed bottles and mirrors in saloons with boulders and bricks. Her husband—David at the time—suggested that a cleaver might be more efficient. It might have been the first time she had agreed with him. The image of Carry A. Nation soon spread: a greying lady, over six feet, with a camp guard's gaze, in black and white clothing, holding a Bible in one hand and an axe in the other. The war against the 'demon drink' had begun.

Against whisky and rum, in the first place.

John Dobson ran a saloon in Kiowa, Kansas, and was visited by an angry Carry in June 1900. Her goal was to smash everything to pieces, and she succeeded in no time at all. Her axe was a very useful tool. Billiard balls and cues also came in handy.

Carry didn't stick just to this saloon. She took care of all the taverns in the street. She was convinced that God was helping her in all of this. Since the saloons were illegal, Carry was not arrested.

Her most famous intervention took place six months later, in Wichita. There, the luxurious Carey Hotel was her target. She caused more than three thousand dollars in damage. All the alcohol, mirrors, tables, and chairs were destroyed, as well as a painting entitled 'Cleopatra in the bath'. While she was also demolishing the bar counter, she was arrested.

Carry was sent to jail. It would be the first time she was arrested of thirty more to come.

She was released on bail after three weeks. But it was enough for her husband David to file for divorce because of 'desertion'.

However, Carry A. Nation would soon be released. Alcohol remained her biggest enemy, but she was also against other temptations, such as tobacco, slot machines, strange dishes, elegant and short clothes, corsets, orders and commands, lustful acts and pharmacies. Pharmacies also sold alcohol.

At the end of her life she made a living by giving lectures and selling her photographs and miniature hatchets. She died in 1911.

At the time, many saloons started displaying signs which read: 'All nations welcome, but Carry'.

33

THE MONARCH OF THE GLEN

WHISKY SAVES ART

The National Galleries of Scotland are the lucky owners of a sublime masterpiece by 19th-century painter Sir Edwin Landseer: The Monarch of The Glen. The work shows a tough and muscled stag, cast in full light against a gloomy, threatening background. The animal exudes grace and strength, dominating the scene: majestic; self-assured; defiant; an unthreatened ruler. Landseer clearly loved these animals.

Yet, Landseer had an even stronger bond with dogs. Newfoundland dogs: those sturdy, large animals best known for their swimming prowess and patience, and often considered indispensable as rescuers of persons from the sea. They are actually called 'Landseer Newfoundland dogs', named after the man who immortalised them in beautiful works, usually in black and white.

But it is because of The Monarch that Sir Edwin Landseer deserves his place in this book. And there is a clear link with whisky.

Landseer painted the canvas in 1851. It didn't get a lot of attention at first, but it was slowly discovered. In 1916 Sir Thomas Dewar bought the painting. The word 'Dewar' should ring a bell with people who love whisky. John Dewar & Sons used the image in the marketing of their whiskies. Glenfiddich also used the image for its labels. You could also find 'The Monarch' on biscuit boxes (Walkers) and soup cans (Baxters). Diageo bought Dewar's in 1997 and sold the business to Bacardi a year later, except for the painting itself. In 2016 the work was put up for sale at Christie's, its value estimated at eight million pounds.

The Scots reacted very quickly. 'The Monarch' should stay in Scotland and they wanted the National Galleries of Scotland to buy the canvas. But the National Galleries of Scotland were unable to cough up that amount. So, Diageo made a big gesture: the company was willing to give four million pounds itself, if the National Galleries of Scotland could raise the other four million.

Thanks to the anonymous donations of a large number of art lovers and a few 'trusts', it became possible to keep 'The Monarch' in Scotland.

You see, whisky can save art.

34

THE KEEPERS OF THE QUAICH

'WATER OF LIFE FOREVER'

The 1980s were not the most successful years for the Scotch whisky industry. All means were sought and used to make Scotland and Scotch whisky known worldwide. Many companies, associations and individuals worked hard to make this happen.

In 1988, the heads of Allied Distillers Ltd, Justerini & Brooks Ltd, The Highland Distilleries Co. Ltd, Robertson & Baxter Ltd, United Distillers and the Chivas and Glenlivet Group came together to create an exclusive, international non-profit club: 'The Keepers of the Quaich'. The intent was to bring together those individuals who made special efforts to promote Scotch whisky. Anywhere in the world.

Coat of arms and motto of the Keepers.

Anyone could apply, including those not directly involved in the industry: writers, journalists, artists etc. New members had to be introduced by existing Keepers. The management committee could accept them if they had a strong CV. At that moment (February 2020) there were 2,817 Keepers from all parts of the world. Anyone who had been a Keeper for more than ten years can become a Master. He or she must demonstrate their special achievements to promote Scotch whisky.

Since the founding of The Keepers of the Quaich, about two hundred people have been given the title. Twice a year, a dinner is held at Blair Castle (in the Scottish county of Perthshire). The ceremonies always begin with the official entry of the Grand Quaich. This Quaich, the symbol of The Keepers of the Quaich, is an exceptionally large silver dish, measuring 62 centimetres from handle to handle. All the decorations on the Quaich refer to whisky. The Keepers' coat of arms is engraved in the bottom of the Quaich. The Quaich is kept in Blair Castle, the seat of the Keepers.

The Keepers' motto 'Uisgebeatha Gu Brath' means 'Water of Life Forever'.

The Duke of Argyll is Grand Master of the Keepers, and among the 'patrons' of the society we find several nobilities, including The Earl of Erroll, Lord High Constable of Scotland, The Duke of Atholl, and The Earl of Hopetoun.

35

THE ATLANTIC CHALLENGE

TALISKER WHISKY RULES THE WAVES

From the town of San Sebastian on La Gomera, one of the Canary Islands, to Nelson's Dockyard in English Harbour on the Carribbean island of Antigua, it is approximately 5,400 kms. Between those two points lies only water: the Atlantic Ocean.

Every year, Talisker Whisky offers you a chance to take this crossing. It's not completely free, and you have to row that distance all by yourself. Yes, rowing across the Atlantic. To make you even more excited, they say this: 'Once you leave the safety of the harbour, you'll be on your own on the vast ocean and at the mercy of the elements, until the race comes into its final stretch!"

The Maclean brothers arriving in Antigua.

It's nothing new: adventurous sports enthusiasts have been trying to row across the ocean since 1966. Not always with great success. Organised crossings gradually emerged, which inevitably turned into competitions. In 2013, Talisker decided to sponsor one of those competitions and make it a biennial event.

In 2015, 26 teams immediately enrolled, twice as many as the first edition. Talisker decided to organise this sporting event annually.

The competition was only a matter of getting to the other side. But you had to abide by the rules. The rules were simple: a maximum of five people could sit in each boat. External help on the journey was not permitted. Boats could only move by rowing, and with some help from ocean currents and wind. You could bring food, but you had to get your water from the ocean.

Furthermore: you had to take all your waste back home with you.

In the Blue Marlin, a bar in San Sebastian where the participants meet in the evening during the weeks of preparation, we find out what else is required.

To start with: a few years of preparation, professional training, and four diplomas, including RYA Yachtmaster Ocean Theory, First Aid at Sea, Sea Survival, and a VHF Radio Licence.

And unavoidably: money! We hear about amounts up to 150,000 pounds sterling to cover registration, rowing boat, and training. You will also need: solar panels; the AIS, which allows you to communicate with other ships; the satellite telephone; the special 'Toughbooks' (laptops that can take more hits than the one in front of me); the GPS; and a desalination machine to make drinking water.

The Dane, Carsten Heron Olsen, CEO of Atlantic Campaigns SL and the Race Director, designs the entire sporting event and follows each participant closely from the start, 24/7:

'Any boat along the way can contact us at any time. We also automatically receive a signal every two hours from each boat from which we can get all the information related to their location, speed, course and so on. In addition, every two days we radio contact each boat to make sure there are no problems and to know where to intervene. There is always a team of specialists ready to give advice on how to solve problems on the boat: from healthcare to technical problems.'

Carsten Heron Olsen believes it's logical that no external help is permitted.

'They need to bring enough food and first aid equipment for 90 days. They have to extract water from the ocean and desalinate it. All spare parts for possible breakdowns must be on board. Anyone who asks for extras along the way will be kicked out of the race. But emergencies can arise that transcend all rules. One of our own sailing ships sails in front of the race, and a ship with technicians and doctors on board follows. In New York, a team of meteorologists, specialising in ocean weather, follows the race day and night, and they can give advice to the rowers. The crossing usually takes between thirty and eighty days.'

For the first time, three brothers rowed across the ocean: Ewan, James, and Lachlan MacLean, sons of whisky writer Charles MacLean. They broke the world record with a time of 35 days, nine hours, and nine minutes. Six days less than the previous record.

WHISKY?
FOR MEN ONLY!

On December 5, 1933, the United States Congress signed the famous '21st Amendment' that ended 'The Noble Experiment' of Prohibition. In the months previous, there had been a lot of debate between supporters and opponents. In November 1933, in order to strengthen their hand, a number of distilleries grouped together to form a syndicate which is now known as the Distilled Spirits Institute. After Prohibition, the Distilled Spirits Institute aimed, among other things, to boost the image of the sector, but also developed a number of rules that the members were required to adhere to in their marketing and promotion.

KING MEANS BEST IN EVERYTHING

Bobsledding . . . King of Winter Sports!

BROWN-FORMAN'S — KING OF PRE-WAR WHISKY*

KING
Blended Whisky

For special moments, there's nothing like smooth, *so* LIGHT *yet* King Whisky. In fine clubs and bars—and at home—more and more discriminating people are enjoying Brown-Forman's King of pre-war whisky—so light, so mellow, and yet so full-flavored and satisfying.

BROWN-FORMAN DISTILLERS CORPORATION
At Louisville in Kentucky

*Blended Whisky, 86 Proof. The straight whiskies in this product are 51 months or more old. 40% straight whiskies; 60% grain neutral spirits.

An important item was about 'advertising'. In order to upset as few people as possible, they were asked to observe the following rules:

1. No advertising via the radio.
2. No advertising in states that were partially 'dry'.
3. No dates or references to events taking place on Sundays.
4. No images or texts addressed to women. 'Men only!'

The Distilled Spirits Institute still exists, but has been part of the Distilled Spirits Council of the United States since 1973.

37

FRANCE'S TREASURED WHISKY

LIBERTÉ, ÉGALITÉ, TULLAMORE DEW

In 2014, William Grant & Sons, owner of Glenfiddich and The Balvenie among others, managed to acquire Tullamore Dew, the Irish whiskey brand. They brought it back from Midleton to their new distillery in Tullamore, a bustling town near the centre of Ireland, where this whiskey originated around 1900.

Let's analyse the brand name: Tullamore refers to the town, but 'dew' has nothing to do with 'morning dew'. They're just the initials of Daniel Edmond Williams, the manager behind the product.

Tullamore Dew was created for the American palate (flavourful, but not too strong, heavy or complex). It has been successful in the USA. But Germany is also a big buyer, and somewhat surprisingly, France. According to experts, this is not only due to 'le gout du

Tullamore Dew under construction.

whisky', but especially to the way in which the French pronounce the name: Not 'Tullamore', but 'Tout l'amour.'

'Tout l'amour' is a much stronger motto for the French than the national "liberté, égalité, fraternité."

38

THANKS TO CASSIS DE DIJON

EUROPE SETS THE RECORD STRAIGHT

If we buy a bottle of whisky anywhere in Europe today, we know for sure that it contains 'whisky'. The fact that this is enforced by a European law we owe to Cassis de Dijon.

Cassis de Dijon, better known as 'Crème de Cassis', is a rather sweet, dark-red berry liqueur from Burgundy. 'Kir' drinkers know it's the base of their beloved aperitif, complemented by a dry white wine.

Cassis de Dijon appeared on the market around 1850, but our story begins in 1976.

At that time, the German importer REWE-Zentral AG applied to the *Bundesmonopolverwaltung* for a license to import Cassis de Dijon into its country. Their application was rejected.

The reason was simple: Cassis de Dijon's alcohol content is less than twenty percent ABV, while fruit liqueurs in Germany must be at least 32 percent ABV. Bad luck.

But REWE-Zentral AG didn't stop there. They went to the Court of Justice of the European Economic Community on the basis that there should be 'free transit of goods and services between Member States' of the EEC.

The court ruled in favour of the importer in 1979: every product lawfully produced in a Member State, marketed in that Member State, and stating the country of origin, should be given free passage. If the legislation of the importing country presupposed other specifications that could prevent this, those specifications could only be considered if they were necessary for the protection of public health (and a few other commercial matters).

The European gates were opened immediately for Cassis de Dijon.

Beverage manufacturers across Europe revolted. Anyone in Europe could consequently imitate other drinks from any other Member State and put the same name on them, without having to consider the composition of the original product.

Europe later realised the blunder and in May 1989 published the European Regulation 1576/98 which listed the 'general regulations concerning the definition, description and presentation of spirit drinks'.

Each Member State had to transpose this regulation into a national law.

In 2008, Regulation 110 appeared, extending the previous one to 46 drinks.

39

THE SHOOGLEBOX
ESSENTIAL TOOL

Drop whisky aficionados at any distillery, let them free, and they'll be irresistibly drawn to the room where those graceful copper stills are located. You must have seen it. The guide on site tortures them for a while with a classic chat about barley, water, and yeast (with the inevitable joke about 'the lucky cows in the area' who get the waste). Then he lets them have a (little too long) look at the mill, in which the malted barley is processed into grist. Personally, I have never seen a beautiful mill in all my life. They are also usually painted in shitty green or in the 'red' of blood that has congealed long ago.

Less attention is paid to a simple wooden container that has been placed there casually: the shooglebox. It's a combination of three trays which fit neatly on top of each other. The top two have a sieve as a base. The sieve of the middle tray is the finest.

The elegance of a mill.

Once crushed, barley consists of three parts: the husk, the grist, and the flour. The grist, which is modified starch, is very important for further production, because that's where we get the sugar. We need the husks as a filter bed in the mash tun, where we will filter the sugars from the crushed grain with hot water. We will then convert those sugars into alcohol. If the filter is too fine, the mash tun will empty too slowly. If the filter is too coarse, everything goes too fast and we lose extracts.

Measuring the proportion between those three parts is the mission. The shooglebox will save us.

You pour a specified amount of ground barley into the top tray, after which you shake well and the three parts are separated: at the top you will find the husk, in the middle the grist, and at the bottom the flour.

The exact ratio varies from distillery to distillery, but it fluctuates around twenty percent husk, seventy percent grist, and ten percent flour.

The inventor of the shooglebox is unknown.

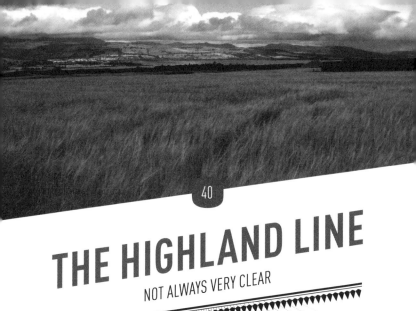

40

THE HIGHLAND LINE

NOT ALWAYS VERY CLEAR

Britons have always had a problem with borders. Crazy, if you live on an island. Water is the border. But the UK is composed of four countries.

Before 1707, for example, no one knew exactly where the boundary lay between the land of the Scots and that of their 'beloved' neighbours, the English. Berwick-upon-Tweed, for instance, belonged to England, according to some, and to Scotland according to others. In that area you can still find a few places where people are still not quite sure.

But we, whisky aficionados, know one boundary for sure: The Highland Line. It divides the Scotch whisky world into the Highlands and the Lowlands. Everything produced above it is 'Highland whisky' and everything created below it is 'Lowland whisky'.

Easy.

It was the Scotch Whisky Association (SWA) that established this boundary line in its 2009 Scotch Whisky Regulations.

But the Highland Line actually runs right through what is (geographically) known as the Lowlands. Above that SWA line, in the whisky Highlands, there is actually still quite a bit of Lowlands. So who cares? It's important to know where the line is, so you know exactly what you're drinking.

Take a look at the map: we start in Greenock, west of Glasgow, and cross the Clyde to Cardross. From Cardross Station we go in a straight line to the highest point of Earl's Seat and from there, again in a straight line, to the Wallace Monument in Stirling. From now on, we follow the road: the B998, then the A91, and finally the M90 until Bridge of Earn. From here we follow the south bank of the River Earn and the River Tay to the North Sea in the east.

Voilà. At least that's to the point.

But don't say this too loudly when a geographer is listening in. Because, according to those guys, the Highland Line is somewhere else. They say that the Line continues from Helensburgh in the west, straight towards Stonehaven in the east. Just past the Cairngorms, it makes a sharp turn to the north to end near Nairn. Aberdeen and the entire area are therefore located in the Lowlands. That's why it takes so long, driving north from Edinburgh, before you see the 'Welcome to the Highlands' sign.

But again: keep it quiet. Otherwise, a historian will tell you that the real Highland Line was precisely drawn in 1784 in the famous Wash Act. That imaginary line follows the geographic boundary, but starts higher in the west, at Loch Crinan. Thanks to that 'border', the government was able to introduce two different tax systems: below the line, where there was less poverty and more legal distilling, the taxes were higher than above the line. They hoped that this might help avoid smuggling and illegal distilling in the Highlands.

So, three Highland Lines! But not one single Scot will care, as long as he knows where the border with those 'bloody' English lies.

41

LIGHT WHISKEY?

OMG!

Do not freak out! We won't talk about diet whiskey. We will, however, talk about whiskey on the American market. During the second half of the last century, the American whiskey world ran into trouble: the demand for bourbon, corn whiskey, and the other classic American whiskeys had fallen alarmingly for several years. The Americans turned to vodka and gin, and even preferred Irish and Scotch whiskeys.

The government intervened and created 'light whiskey'. The Code of Federal Regulations (the official list of all liquor definitions) states: 'Light whiskey is a distillate or a blend of distillates, distilled after January 26, 1968, to more than 80 and less than 95 percent ABV, whether or not aged in used barrels or unroasted new oak barrels.' This whiskey is lighter in taste and lighter in colour, but not in calories.

Didn't we learn that whiskey in America may not be distilled higher than eighty percent ABV? And didn't we learn that a barrel can be used only once in America?

We ask the TTB, the Alcohol and Tobacco Tax and Trade Bureau, which takes care of all taxes on trade and importation of alcohol: 'A distillate, based on a grain mash, distilled to a maximum of 95 percent ABV, that, which has the aroma and characteristics normally expected from whiskey, and which has been bottled at minimum forty percent ABV, is whiskey."

Let's double-check in the Code of Federal Regulations (which writes "whisky" without an e, by the way). 'Bourbon whisky', 'Rye whisky', 'Wheat whisky', 'Malt whisky', and 'Corn whisky' may not be distilled higher than eighty percent ABV and the barrels used must always be brand new barrels.

The fact that the definition clearly says 'new' is, according to some, due to considerable lobbying by the Unions, although it was already an unwritten agreement between coopers and distillers shortly after the Prohibition.

BAKERY HILL DISTILLERY

AUSTRALIA'S 'LAST' AND 'FIRST' DISTILLERY

In 1921, Edinburgh Distillers Company Limited (DCL) built a brand-new distillery in Geelong, just outside Melbourne, Victoria: the Corio Distillery. It was one of the biggest in the world. According to Australian whisky connoisseurs, at that time, the DCL motto was: 'Making a whisky not better than the worst whisky in Scotland'. And they were right. DCL's Corio and Bond 7 blends weren't for the faint of heart and their Corio 5 Star Whisky was quickly nicknamed COR-10, referring to a gasoline brand. A Corio with cola was the cheapest drink in the entire state of Victoria.

In 1989 Corio closed Australia's last working distillery. Every Australian was convinced that Australia was not a good place to make whisky. At the end of the last century, David Baker, a specialist in microbiology and biochemistry, gave up his teaching job.

He was convinced that Australian whisky was fine, as long as you ensured quality. With all the money he had, he bought a building on the outskirts of Melbourne and had a small still made by the English John Doran Company (which also built the very first column still for inventor Aeneas Coffey). His goal was good Australian malt whisky.

'This is Australia's very first distillery,' he said proudly when we first met. 'What about Tasmania?' I asked carefully. 'Tasmania isn't Australia!' he replied shortly, but changed his mind quickly. 'It's better not to write that. Those guys over there don't like that. Write that I said "mainland".'

People liked the name of his new distillery: Bakery Hill. Bakery refers to David's family name and Hill refers to where the distillery is located, at the foot of Mount Dandenong, a heavy hill.

Bakery Hill is one of the country's most iconic historic sites. It is a small neighbourhood near the town of Ballarat, not far from the distillery.

During the gold rush, in the 1850s, many English fortune seekers (mainly from Cornwall) emigrated to Victoria, hoping to find gold. The Australian government immediately introduced a 'search tax', a mandatory license (one pound per six months): the 'miners right'. That was a lot of money for the small gold that was found there at the time. The government called in the army after the gold miners refused to pay.

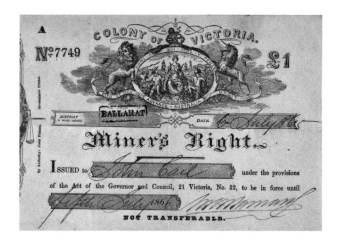

On December 3, 1854, British colonial forces attacked a group of protesters on Bakery Hill. The prospectors built a barricade, designed their own flag on the spot, instantly founded their own state, and declared their independence.

But they were too weak to resist. At least 27 miners were killed in the battle. The remaining prospectors were captured. History books refer to the battle as the Eureka Stockade.

There was overwhelming support for the miners. The entire population in Melbourne and the surrounding area protested. The government had no choice but to grant certain rights, and even voting rights, to the male miners. Women had to wait another five years.

David assured me that he chose the name Bakery Hill only as a tribute to the prospectors.

But I also learned from David that four years after the uprising, the Welcome Nugget was found in the same neighbourhood: a gold nugget with a weight of about seventy kilograms.

Could this have been an omen for the Gold Awards awaiting Bakery Hill Distillery?

43

THE MAN WITH THE RED SOCKS

AND AUSTRALIAN WHISKY

There are a number of individuals that are indispensable to the world of Scotch whisky. These living monuments include: David Stewart of The Balvenie; Richard Paterson at Whyte and Mackay; Jim McEwan, formerly of Bruichladdich, now with Ardnahoe; and Ronnie Cox, to name only a few.

Anyone who has ever attended a masterclass by Ronnie Cox will know what 'enthusiasm' is for the rest of his or her life. He, like the *Pied Piper of Hamelin*, effortlessly led everyone straight to the nearest bottle of Glenrothes, for which he was then 'Brands Heritage Director'. He put Glenrothes, a fantastic vintage whisky, in the spotlight around the world.

He is also known (among insiders) for his extensive wardrobe. Jim McEwan once called him 'the best dressed man in Scotland'.

Cox's legendary tasting table.

However, only a few outsiders are aware of his extra quirk: He has been wearing red stockings his entire life. He has a legitimate reason for that. In his family tree you will find John Comyn III of Badenoch, better known as Red Comyn, because of his hair colour.

Red Comyn was from a Flemish family and played an important role in the first war of independence. He even claimed the throne after that. But he didn't make it because he was murdered in 1296 by the future King Robert the Bruce. The Scots always wore red stockings in the battle during those wars. That way, an injured leg could bleed profusely without the enemy noticing. Better they don't know where your weaknesses are.

Ronnie's red stockings are therefore a tribute to his 'red' ancestor.

RONNIE THE SAVIOUR

What's even less known: Ronnie saved the Australian drinks world from fatal ruin. Around 2003, after twenty bad years for the drinks industry, the Australian government wanted to relax the legislation related to the production of spirits.

In particular, the existing obligation to mature whisky, rum, and brandy for at least two years would disappear.

Ronnie at work.

A number of distilleries, who wanted to get their alcohol into the bottle faster, were enthusiastic proponents. The world turned more and more to gin, vodka, and the alcopops that were more easily produced than whisky.

Everyone in the whisky business understood that this change in the law would make it possible for all kinds of products to be imported. Even drinks which were produced legally or illegally anywhere, and which would carry a label that didn't even refer to the contents.

That might have been fatal for many whisky-producing countries.

But it didn't get that far.

The Australians owe this to one man: Ronnie Cox. He managed to convince several Scottish distillers to join his protest and to lobby the Australian legislators collectively.

The Australians eventually tied up.

We asked Ronnie for comment.

'I remember those conversations in Canberra well,' he laughs. 'Basically, I just wanted to make it clear to them that Australian whiskies would have had a much better future internationally if they were also aged for three years, just like Scotch whisky. And they did it.'

44

TAIWAN

STRONG RISER

In Taiwan, it was ear-splittingly quiet on the whisky front, unlike in Japan where the industry had been booming for a long time. When we compare the countries' whisky histories, there is a clear difference. 1923: first whisky at Yamazaki in Japan. 2006: first whisky at Kavalan in Taiwan. Barley grows well in Japan. There is very little barley in Taiwan. But that's not the real reason.

In 1901, when the Japanese occupied Taiwan, they established a state company that controlled just about everything that could be controlled: The Monopoly Bureau of the Taiwan Governor's Office. That company had the monopoly on the production and sale of cigarettes, wines, beers, distillates and petroleum products. Even the standardization of weights and measures was decided by that Bureau.

After World War II, Taiwan was ruled by the Chinese nationalists who took over the office. They renamed it The Taiwan Provincial Monopoly Bureau. The objectives remained the same as before. Wines and spirits are still not allowed to be produced or imported in Taiwan.

噶瑪蘭
單一麥芽威士忌

Kavalan Distillery.

Swaping cards with Mr Y.T.Lee, CEO King Car Co, and Ian Chang, former master distiller at Kavalan.

It wasn't until 1987 before the government finally allowed 'foreign' wines to enter the island. The Taiwanese had to wait until 1991 for whisky from Scotland and the United States. Production of their own whisky was still not allowed. In 2002, the Taiwanese wanted to join the World Trade Organization, but they were told that they had to review some laws first. The Taiwan Provincial Monopoly Bureau deleted a number of regulations and changed its name to Taiwan Tobacco and Liquor Corporation, abbreviated to TTL. That's why the Taiwanese could only dream about their 'own' whisky since the end of 2001. But nobody was prepared for that at the time. Not even the TTL.

Mr T.T. Lee, a Taiwanese businessman who had set up a company years previously that marketed instant coffee, managed to expand his business into a blockbuster across diverse sectors: from orchids to insecticides. Mr T.T. Lee, a collector of vintage cars, named the company King Car Company. He already had plans for a distillery in 2001, but the real construction only started in April 2005. Eight months later, the job was done. On March 11, 2006, at exactly 8.30 in the evening, the first drop of Taiwanese new spirit entered the spirit safe: Kavalan whisky was ready to conquer the world.

It took until 2008 before TTL came out with whisky: blended malts, which mainly contained Scotch whisky. In the meantime, there was plenty of distillation, and in 2018 the TTL announced its own single-malt whisky for the first time: Omar. In the meantime, Kavalan had already worked its way into the top ten world whiskies.

45

63.4 = 111
THE MYSTERIOUS NUMBER

Is it a tradition or a well-thought-out strategic move? No idea. Since time immemorial, most distilleries have reduced the Alcohol By Volume (ABV) of the newly distilled spirit to 63.4% before entering the barrel.

Why exactly 63.4%?

I once asked my late friend Jan Filliers, then master distiller at Filliers in Belgium, who always adhered to that rule.

'Because my grandfather told me so,' was his reply.

Put the question in Scotland and you're guaranteed to get the answer: 'Because you get a better interaction between the alcohol and the wood. Whisky matures better at 63.4.'

But let us take two identical barrels. We fill them both with the same new spirit at 63.4% ABV, and leave them side by side, for let's say, ten years. I bet we will find two different whiskies as a result. So, allow me to doubt the previous Scottish answer we received.

Let us try again somewhere else in Scotland: 'Because newly filled barrels were and are often exchanged between distilleries and bottlers. If everyone fills at 63.4, then you don't have to make annoying calculations between the different alcohol levels.'

Sounds very logical, and that is perhaps the most plausible explanation.

But the question remains: why 63.4? That's not the easiest number to remember, is it? I think a nicely rounded 60 would be better, right?

But wait a minute. ABV – Alcohol By Volume – is a fairly modern measure. In the past, distillers worked with 'proof'. To know the relationship between the two, just multiply ABV by 1.75 to get your degree proof.

Now look: 63.45 multiplied by 1.75 gives you 111.

Tadaaa. There is no easier number to remember.

That's why we agree with the last answer, but with 'proof' in mind.

Unfortunately, there are no certainties in the whisky world.

In America, 63.4 ABV equals 126.8 degrees proof. They don't multiply by 1.75, they just double it. New spirits can be stored there up to a maximum of 62.5% ABV, or 125 degrees proof.

But new spirits in Scotland and America nowadays regularly exceed the ideal levels in the barrel.

It's understandable: if you mature new spirits at 63.4% in a full barrel of two hundred and fifty litters, then 36.6% of your barrel is filled with water. And trust me, water really doesn't mature. An expensive investment.

美味　滋養　葡萄酒

赤玉ポートワイン

46

JAPANESE NUDE

JAPANESE STANDARDS

Shinjiro Torii was born in 1870 in Japan. He worked in his uncle's shop as a teenager, crafting and selling 'healthy' drinks. Maybe this was the reason for his later interest in European wines and spirits. He started selling wine when he was twenty; mostly wine from Spain.

But it was a complete flop. It wasn't necessarily his fault, or the fault of the wine, but perhaps it had something to do with the customer. The taste of the Japanese is very different from the Europeans: Japanese find Spanish wines much too sour, much too bitter, not sweet enough, and difficult to drink.

Shinjiro was aware of the problem. He used the experience from his early childhood to create a Spanish wine that was more 'drinkable'. With a selection of ingredients, he transformed Spanish wine into a very sweet, fruity wine liqueur, which he marketed in 1907 under the name Akadama Port Wine.

Fifty years later, the Portuguese were angry. The government wanted the word Port to disappear from the label. But Torii wasn't concerned. The Japanese loved his 'Port'. He kept the name until 1973, when he was forced to change the name to Akadama Red Wine.

In the meantime, he learned a lot about marketing and advertising from another uncle.

In 1922, Shinjiro Torii knocked on the door of one of Osaka's top advertising executives: Kataoka. He had an idea for a striking advertising campaign.

For this campaign, Kataoka invited Emiko Matsushima to model. Emiko was a well-known opera star and actress who also acted in some silent films. The photographer on the campaign, Turo Kawashima, spent a whole week shooting photos. He took more than a hundred shots of Emiko holding a glass of Akadama Port Wine in her hand.

Emiko posed initially in a kimono, but after a few days she modelled in her 'négligée'. And finally, she posed naked. Or at least what the Japanese considered to be naked.

At that time in Japanese culture, the most reprehensible thing a woman could do was show her bare shoulder. A bare shoulder made it onto Kataoka's poster, eventually making it into the market a year later.

In the meantime, the idea of distilling whisky had grown among the Japanese. But it was still a niche industry. According to Shinjiro Torii and many of his business friends, it was a craft better left to the Scots and Irish. "Even if I had a lot of money," said Torii, "I wouldn't make whisky."

TONDEMONAI, OUTSTANDING!

The 'naked' Emiko looks on innocently from a dark, sepia background. You can see that both of her shoulders are bare. She holds a glass of sparkling red wine in her hand. At the bottom of the poster, there's a simple slogan: 'Delicious, nutritious, easy... Akadama Port Wine.'

Cue outrage everywhere.

Emiko's family wanted nothing more to do with her.

Later, when she would visit Torii's offices, a shouting crowd was waiting for her. Even the police took her aside for a brief interrogation.

But inside Torii's office, the cash was flying in. Akadama Port Wine became and continues to be an unsurpassed success. With the proceeds of his Red Wine, Shinjiro Torii, despite his former oath, started his own whisky distillery in Osaka in 1924: Yamazaki.

He later linked the name Suntory to it: 'Sun' referring to the red sphere on his old wine bottles and 'Tory', the link to his name.

Now Suntory Beverage & Food Limited has grown into one of the largest producers of spirits in the world.

Who said nude doesn't sell?

DOMECQ
Alexander Fleming
June 10 '48
DOMECQ
5-I-55
DOMECQ
7-Julio-1953
DOMECQ
F. Jardiel Poncela
Febrero 1944
DOMECQ
Wellington
y
Ciudad Rodrigo
DOMECQ
Paloma Picasso
27.9.86
With my best
wishes and
thanks!
Charlton Heston
4.5.75

47

SHERRY BUTTS
A SPANISH FAIRY TALE?

Ten years ago, I walked through the wonderful art collection of Bodegas Tradicion in Jerez de la Frontera. Art in a bodega? Yes. Picasso, Goya, and others. Worth the journey! The real purpose of the trip was to see the warehouses of this unique sherry producer. In the warehouse, surrounded by black-painted solero casks, neatly stacked four rows high, we persuaded cellar master Pepe Blandino to allow us fifteen minutes.

Blandino is in charge of the wine production on a daily basis. He might be able to rid me of my doubts about sherry casks. My main questions: what about 'Scottish' sherry butts? Are those barrels really made of Spanish oak?

How fruitful can fifteen minutes be, even if you find yourself amidst the top sherries of the world? 'We don't use Spanish oak,' said Blandino. 'Spanish oak is far too difficult to work with. And you must know: sherry breaks down in Spanish oak. All barrels in the bodegas are American oak. The Spanish law requires this, by the way.'

Blandino was more liberal with his adjectives when we tasted, but that didn't stop him from entrusting me with more of these carefully crafted samples.

'No bodega uses new barrels,' he said. 'When an extra barrel enters the bodega cellar, it is first filled with sherry, and that sherry remains in it for as long as possible, sometimes up to ten years. Only then, when the barrel is completely saturated, it is emptied, and the sherry used is processed into sherry vinegar. Only after that can a barrel enter the cellar. The barrel will be painted black with a special pigment. That prevents bacteria from getting in, but it does let the oxygen through."

Unlike in the whisky world, Jerez producers don't want a barrel to have a hold on the taste of the wine. By 'waiting' for about ten years before entering the warehouse, the barrel has lost enough of its strength to interact with the alcohol. And that makes them happy.

Sherry makers in Jerez only want the wine to have enough oxygen to ferment. The whisky industry would never ask for such a 'lazy' cask.

'Once in the cellar, the barrel never comes out again,' says Blandino. 'We have barrels that are a hundred years old, and here in Jerez there are casks that are twice as old.'

'SCOTTISH' SHERRY BARRELS

The English have been avid sherry drinkers for a long time. They've always imported large quantities of sherry, especially during the seventeenth century. That sherry was delivered in barrels of Spanish oak by the Spaniards. Those casks were only made for transport. Once a barrel was empty, it was cheaper to make a new one in Spain than to transport an old one back to Spain.

In the next century, the drinking habits of the English changed. They switched to port. William III of Orange was the person responsible for this. He was married to Mary, daughter of James VII, the exiled king of Scotland and England. William III was Dutch and he imported jenever and port.

Sherry casks in a bodega.

Sherry production and distribution progressed again in the nineteenth century. Sherry barrels arrived in huge quantities.

They stayed in England as before, and the distillers were happy to use them. In 1946 the Spanish government complained that this was not the right way to work. It was not until 1985 that a law was passed banning the export of sherry in barrels.

Meanwhile, the demand for sherry in England had diminished, and after some years, there was a glaring shortage of Spanish barrels. There was no other choice but to order those barrels yourself in Spain.

Jerez now has four coopers, and they are very busy. They work almost exclusively for the whisky industry. They produce mainly 500 litre butts, but in European oak. In the past we would have written 'in Spanish oak'. Most of the oak used now comes from the former Eastern Bloc countries.

These brand-new barrels are temporarily filled with must (the intermediate step between grape juice and wine) or with sherry of slightly lesser quality. Or with paxarette.

Once marinated, the 'sherry' cask is ready for whisky.

Sherry casks in a whisky distillery.

WHERE IS THE TIME OF THE PAXARETTE?

In Henri IV, Shakespeare has his protagonist exclaim, 'If I had a thousand sons, the first human principle I would teach them would be to renounce bland potions and become addicted to sack.'

By 'sack' he meant (we think) a then common 'wine', which probably only later received the name paxarette, or pajarete in Spanish.

Paxarette is a mixture of a sweet light wine with a concentrated decoction of must. In short: colourful and very sweet. Until the end of the eighteenth century, the English were only too happy to drink paxarette.

The stuff was good for other things as well. Just before transport, new barrels that had to be sent to the United Kingdom from Spain were filled with litres of the substance. The vessel was pressurised so that the paxarette could spread quickly. Along the way, the paxarette was given enough time to marinate the barrel by sloshing around in it.

Because some distillers 'forgot' to take the paxarette out before filling the cask with whisky, its use was banned around 1990.

48

DEVIL'S SHARE
THE ANGELS MISS OUT

David Lloyd George, a British minister, decided in 1915 that whisky should be kept in a barrel for three years. Europe is still bound by that rule. Fortunately, sixty to seventy percent of the taste and smell in your glass comes from that barrel.

We have to pay a heavy toll for this: everyday, part of the contents of the barrel evaporate. New oxygen enters as alcohol and water escapes. But don't worry. This gives an extra boost to the silent orgy that takes place all the time in the barrel: an enriching lovemaking between alcohol, wood, and oxygen. This doesn't change the fact that the distiller watches with sadness as the amount of liquid in his barrels decreases.

The government, benevolent as always, does take this into account. The distillery can charge a loss of two percent each year. We are among the 'lucky'.

The evaporation depends on several factors: the climate, the humidity, the location. In Victoria (Australia), for example, the loss is four percent. It is usually so dry there that it is especially the water that escapes from the barrel, much more than the alcohol. This means that the contents of the barrel decrease, but the alcohol content increases. In wetter areas we get the opposite. There, more alcohol disappears than water.

Kavalan, in the Yilan Plain on Taiwan's east coast, is reporting an evaporation rate of nearly 15 percent, while the Nantou Distillery in central and higher Taiwan is counting only on seven percent.

◆ Escaping vapors.

At Kavalan, a barrel is empty after seven years! But on the other hand, it takes less time for the maturation to produce beautiful whiskies. In Nantou, distillation is only feasible during the 'winter' because the temperatures make it impossible in the other seasons.

The escaping ethanol vapours are romantically referred to as 'the angels' share'! The French call it 'la part des anges'.

But it's nonsense! The molecular weight of ethanol is almost twice as much as air. Ethanol is heavier than air. And heavier means descending, not ascending! So those alcohol vapours never reach the angels.

They already have rice pudding with golden spoons anyway.

MIND YOUR HEAD

49

AIRCRAFT TASTING

STAY ON THE GROUND

During a whisky tasting, it's all about tastes and smells. Not that we have really good tools for that! In terms of taste, we can distinguish no more than five basic tastes: sweet, salty, sour, bitter, and umami.

Our smell is better, however. Apparently, we can distinguish more than thirty thousand aromas. But only four percent of all the air that enters our nose passes past that olfactory epithelium, a postage stamp in size, which has to decompose everything.

Not very impressive. Not on land, not at sea, and certainly not in the air. When someone offers you an exclusive whisky tasting on an airplane? Then report in sick.

Changed air pressure and the humidity levels in airplanes have an unexpected impact on our sense of taste. The Finnish airline Finnair, among others, has done a lot of research into this. Even the noise of the engines affects taste.

Once in the air, we taste less sweet, less sour, less bitter, and remarkably less salty. That is why airplane meals always contain much more salt. You can't taste it up there, but it would stand out on the ground. Accordingly, it's better not to order a Caol Ila whisky, with its subtle saltiness, on an airplane, if you ever get that chance.

Only umami, the fifth and 'youngest' taste, which the Japanese chemist Kikunae Ikeda was only able to detect in seaweed in 1908, seems to be unaffected by the entire flight experience.

You can find umami, which means 'delicious taste' in Japanese, in salmon, soy sauce, tomato, and ginger. But it is difficult to describe. Plain: not sweet, not salty, not sour, not bitter, but delicious.

Tomato juice, for instance, is full of umami, which is perhaps why a bloody mary is one of the most requested cocktails on airplanes.

50

SINGLE MALT, PURE MALT

VATTED MALT, BLENDED MALT, BLENDED WHISKY

It's hard not to get lost in the maze of whisky types. The reason is very simple: some type names are so confusing they are hard to understand, and other names shouldn't be used anymore.

Of course, for you, as a whisky afficianado, there is no problem. Sure? Let's list them anyway.

Malt means (in short) made from malted barley. Grain whisky is (to put it briefly) distilled from a mixture of grains. Single malt means all alcohol in the bottle is made from malted barley in one and the same distillery (hence 'single'). Pure malt, vatted malt, and blended malt all indicate that the alcohol in the bottle is made from malted barley at different distilleries and then blended.

That is where the misunderstanding begins: blending and vatting do not always mean the same thing in all English-speaking countries. In most countries, vatting involves putting together several malts, whether or not they're from the same distillery. But in some countries, it can also mean that several grain whiskies are mixed, whether or not they're from the same distillery. Meanwhile, blending means the mixing of malt and grain whiskies, whether or not they're from the same distillery. In Ireland, however, blending and vatting are synonyms.

Can you see the storm coming?

CARDHU STARTED IT ALL

It all started with the marketing of Cardhu Pure Malt Speyside Scotch Whisky by Diageo in 1982. Prior to that, you could get Cardhu Single Malt Scotch Whisky, labelled '12 year', in every good liquor store. All the whisky in that bottle was distilled at Cardhu distillery.

In 1982, there was a major problem for the company: There wasn't enough 12-year-old Cardhu in stock. Accordingly, the Diageo mixed malts from some of its other distilleries in Speyside with some Cardhu malt. They put the stuff in the same bottle as before, and pretty much stuck the same label on it. Only those who looked closely at the small print noticed that 'single malt' had been changed into 'pure malt'. The Scotch Whisky Association (SWA) immediately intervened because they believed that the word 'pure' gave the impression to the buyer that the whiksy was better than 'single malt'.

In 2009, the SWA decided that the expressions 'pure malt' and 'vatted malt' couldn't be used in Scotland any longer. They were to be replaced by 'blended malt'. This is upheld in The Scotch Whisky Regulations 2009, published by the Scotch Whisky Association and adopted by the Scottish Government.

Consequently, in Scotch whisky, you will find only single malt, blended malt, and blended whisky. But not in the rest of the world.

After the publication of that Act, there were murmurs throughout the whisky community. After all, that decision could cause a lot of confusion in other countries and put the whiskies that were produced there in a vulnerable position.

Wouldn't the SWA have been aware of that?

Ronnie Cox was a member of the decision-making committee. He travels all over the world, and knows better than anyone that fake bottles with ridiculous names are to be found everywhere. Let's call Ronnie Cox.

Ronnie: 'Yeah, this was at that SWA general meeting in Edinburgh in 2009. We were split into different groups to discuss specific topics. One of these points was the proposed change in definitions. I was sitting in the front row, listening to the speaker who suggested replacing vatted malt with blended malt.'

'Fifty persons from the whisky industry were looking at me when I asked to speak. I argued that this change would cause significant consumer confusion and damage Scotch whisky as a whole. I was so confident that I asked the audience if those who wanted to keep the "vatted" descriptor would raise their hand. I was surprised and disappointed that only one person did it. Today, you only need to visit China or Taiwan to notice how they juggle terms like 'pure', 'vatted', and 'blended'. This wrong decision by the SWA has done untold damage to one of the most interesting, exciting sectors of the Scotch Whisky industry.'

IT ALL STARTED AROUND 1830

Aeneas Coffey, an Irish excise officer, applied for a patent in 1830 for his revolutionary new still. He was able to continuously distil alcohol, to a very high alcohol content, using cereals other than malted barley.

In addition to the old-fashioned malt alcohol, a completely different and much cheaper grain alcohol was born. But both types of alcohol had different excise duties. Consequently, mixing them was forbidden. In 1860, the excise duties for both types of alcohol were equalized, and mixing malt alcohol with grain alcohol became an accepted reality.

Brian Kinsman, master blender at The Balvenie.

This is how blending was born. Blended whisky was an immediate success. By mixing the two alcohols, the master blender was able to give new accents to malt whisky.

The new drink was cheaper than malt whisky, and the blender was able to keep the same colour and taste for every new batch. Blended whisky still accounts for more than 85 percent of Scottish whisky sales.

Oddly enough, the Irish did not take advantage of their compatriot's invention and initially did not work with the patent still. Due to a lack of grain alcohol, they would not benefit from the success of the blended whiskies for many years.

And then you have the key question: are blended whiskies better than malt whiskies? Or vice versa? There are great whiskies everywhere. Your list will undoubtedly differ from that of your neighbour. But there's nothing wrong with that. That's the true virtue of whisky.

Let's stick to the words of Samuel Bronfman, founder of Canadian Seagram, once one of the largest alcohol distillers in the world: 'Distilling is a science, blending is an art.'

51

1494

WAS JAMES IV AN ALCOHOLIC?

Some years are etched in every Briton's memory. 1066 is one of them: the Battle of Hastings, when England became Norman. 1707 is yet another: the year when the English and Scottish Parliaments became one, even though four hundred years earlier the Scots had sworn that 'as long as but a hundred of us remain alive, never will we on any conditions be brought under English rule.'

Any whisky fan that is worthy of the name will never forget 1494.

The first written mention linking malt and aqua vitae (whisky) was written in that year. It is clearly stated in the Exchequer Rolls, the 'cash book' of the king.

'By the King's Order, eight "bolls" of malt for Brother John Cor to make aqua vitae.' John Cor, mentioned earlier in this book, was the Brother Distiller of Lindores Abbey in the Scottish

region of Fife. The king who ordered the whisky was none other than James IV. According to experts, Brother Cor would have distilled about 250 litres of alcohol with those eight 'bolls' of malt.

Was James IV such a boozer? According to the historians, he didn't flinch when he was offered a glass, but we dare not label him as a drunkard. He was interested in other fields that needed alcohol.

For instance, he was a big fan of medicine. In medicine, alcohol can be useful. His passion was pulling teeth. Whether it was necessary or not, if he could remove a tooth from you, you would make fourteen shillings. The king was even willing to pay double if he were allowed to proceed to extensive blood-letting. Broken legs or arms? James IV was ready.

⬩ King James IV.

He was attracted to technology as well. Flying, for example. Doctor Damien knocked on the king's door, asking to sponsor his project. The king accepted.

Doctor Damien wanted to fly off the walls of Stirling Castle with homemade wings. The experiment was a failure.

James said it was due to the fact that the idiot had used chicken feathers.

'Have you ever seen chickens fly?' he asked.

James was very interested in more. Gunpowder, for instance.

Charles MacLean writes in his fantastic book 'Scotch Whisky. A Liquid History', that Brother Cor received fifteen more orders for aqua vitae, from the king, between 1494 and 1512.

Only one of them had an extra order concerning glasses. People with bad intentions would immediately judge that the aqua vitae was intended for consumption. Definitely not us, because all orders were described as intended for gunpowder and 'other experiments'.

Both were in line with James IV's way of life. He was a persistent gambler and had many mistresses. He strategically placed the ladies near the routes he had to travel during his many pilgrimages to the shrines.

Is 1494 the year when the first mention of 'water of life' was made? We know that the Scots are not the inventors of distilling. Nor are the Irish. The knowledge of distillation, like such a good deal of other wisdom, was born in the East. It was thanks to the Moors that science spread to the west and finally reached our lands.

Distillation was mentioned in a number of writings before 1400, but not directly linked to alcohol.

Arnoldus de Villa Nova is one of the people we came across in our search for the year of the first mention of distilling. He lived between 1240 and 1311 and was known as a doctor, chemist, and astrologer. He also studied physics and philosophy. He wrote several books (almost all of which were published centuries later) and in one of these books he talked more thoroughly about the distillation of wine. He was able to make pure alcohol and was the first to use alcohol as a disinfectant. The fact that he said the world would end in 1378 doesn't mean he drank alcohol. But we don't know that about brother Cor either.

Anyway, who gets the credit for the first mention of distilling now? You decide.

Glencoe, Scotland at its best.

52

THE 9.09% RULE
CANADIAN WHISKY

Better a good neighbour than a distant friend?

Not always. For example, let's take a look at rye whiskey.

Both the US and Canada are well known for it. But the two creations are quite different.

First the US.

We turn to the famous Alcohol and Tobacco Tax and Trade Bureau (TTB) once more. TTB clearly says (but in more words) that rye whiskey must be distilled from a mixture of cereals which contain at least 51% rye, and that distillation cannot be higher than 80 percent ABV. The alcohol must mature (for a short time or longer) in a newly fired cask, with a maximum of 62.5% ABV. The whiskey must hold at least forty percent alcohol by volume in the bottle. If the whiskey in the bottle is less than four years old, it must be stated on the bottle. Adding colouring and/or flavourings is not allowed.

And now across the border into Canada.

Canadian whisky, Canadian rye whiskey, or rye whiskey (three different names for the same thing) is, according to Canada's Food and Drug Regulations, 'a drinkable distillate that has the character, aroma and taste you would normally expect from Canadian whisky.' The regulations continue: 'Adding caramel as a colouring agent and flavouring agents to the end product is possible. The whiskey must be aged in a cask for at least three years and then bottled at a minimum of 40% ABV.'

Strange, isn't it? Apparently, rye isn't required. Obviously, it's enough that the whiskey tastes like rye, without rye having been deployed in production. But even weirder are those "flavourings." What does this mean?

Regulation SI/2009-61, concerning 'Certificates of Age and Origin for Distilled Spirits Produced or Packaged in Canada', clarified the matter when it was published on 1 July 2009.

THE 9.09 RULE

The regulation makes it clear: 'Flavouring is any spirit or wine, domestic or imported, that is at least two years old...'

OK, so you can just add a shot of rum, a fifteen-year-old bottle of Glenfarclas, or a Château Mouton Rothschild, but no new spirit or vodka. But remember: the finished product should still have the character, aroma, and taste of Canadian whisky. Whatever that means. Thankfully, the tastes differ.

Since July 2009, there is a limit on how much can be added: a maximum of 9.09% of the mixture may be 'flavouring'. That is the eleventh part of the bottle. To make it completely vague, that only applies to exported products. But not always: only if the importer wants a 'certificate'. If no certificate is requested, then, just like for Canadian whisky sold in Canada, the 9.09% rule does not apply, and you can mix unruffled. 'Canadian Whisky' may stay on the label. No problem.

As long as the whisky has the character, the aroma... whatever.

53

TEAPOT WHISKY

... FOR A RAINY DAY

Nowadays, employees of a range of different companies drive around in company cars, on electric bicycles, and on other modern conveniences which are provided for free (or as good as) by the employer.

It used to be very different.

In the whisky industry, a perk was always close by. One tradition sadly lost is that of labour being interrupted a few times a day so employees could knock down a 'wee dram'.

Glengoyne distillery in Scotland had a golden rule stating that all employees were entitled to 'three fingers of whisky three times a day'. That whisky was traditionally taken from a first-fill Oloroso cask.

🍷 Glegoyne distillery.

And, of course, always at cask strength. If you hold your hand upright, 'three fingers' is quite a lot. But even if you hold the fingers horizontal, 'three fingers' remains a serious 'dram'.

Child labour was still very common in those days. Children stood with sticks at the washback to keep the foam off the brew. Those three 'wee drams' were a bit too much for them. But there was a solution so their leftover whisky wouldn't be wasted.

There was a teapot on the windowsill in the still room, where young inexperienced employees could put their excess whisky.

It's a kind of first aid boiler for more experienced personnel. This honourable tradition lasted until 1970.

Glengoyne still releases new versions of their 'Teapot Dram', which still uses a first-fill Oloroso cask, in tribute to the ancient custom.

Great. All of us have to honour those traditions.

ELIJAH CRAIG
FATHER OF THE CHARRED CASKS

Heaven Hill Distilleries in Kentucky sells one of its whiskeys under an unusual name: Elijah Craig. The name probably doesn't mean much to those outside the U.S. state, but in Kentucky it's pronounced with reverence. Craig created what is now known as bourbon whiskey. We might call him the "father of bourbon."

But some historians don't think that is true.

Let's tone it down a bit: he was the first to age his whiskey in charred barrels. It's said that Craig gave bourbon a softer taste and a different color.

Who was he and how did he do it?

Born in Orange County, Virginia, in 1738, Craig was a Baptist minister who had previously held many other jobs, including teacher, financier, and distiller. But, he didn't have a license to preach and so he got into trouble quite frequently. He moved to Fayette County, which is now Scott County in Kentucky.

Craig started his distillery there around 1789. Soon afterwards, there was a fire in the barn where he kept empty barrels. Part of it caught fire, but the building was saved.

The inside was damaged and some barrels were burned. Nevertheless, Craig was forced to use those burnt barrels because he had so much new spirit at the distillery. Months later, he discovered that the whiskey from those burnt barrels had a much better color and a softer taste than the others.

Ta-da... So maybe we should call him the 'father of the charred barrels'.

But there are holes in the story.

Isn't it odd that those barrels only caught fire on the inside, and not on the outside? Maybe there's an explanation for that. Check with Gary, a cooper friend at the Speyside Cooperage in Craigellachie, Scotland.

Gary hesitates: 'If alcohol had been in that barrel for a while before the fire, it could be that the inside, where alcohol had penetrated, caught fire first.'

That reduces our doubt. But...

'Listen, to make a barrel you need staves,' says Gary. 'They must be elastic in order to be able to bend when assembling the vessel. Therefore, a fire is always made in the barrel. It could very well be that this cooper 'invented' charring, when he forgot to put out the fire.'

We will stick with that.

Anyway, Elijah Craig became a very prosperous entrepreneur and Elijah Craig Bourbon Whiskey was and still is very popular among Americans.

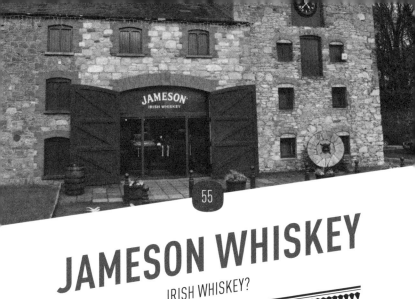

55

JAMESON WHISKEY

IRISH WHISKEY?

Is there anything more Irish than Jameson Whiskey? I would doubt that. Jameson is, by miles, the best-selling Irish blended whiskey. There are more than 90 million bottles sold each year. The distillery in Cork is running at full capacity. And there are many other delicacies made there.

Irish people should be very proud of John Jameson, the man who started it all.

Few people in Ireland know that John Jameson was... a Scotsman. He married a girl from Scotland, Margaret Haig, the eldest daughter of John Haig and Margaret Stein. The names Haig and Stein are well known in the world of Scotch whisky.

Twenty-eight-year-old John married Margaret in 1768. He was then working as a clerk in Clackmannanshire, the Scottish county near Alloa, where he had been born. But he didn't like it, and he moved to Ireland, where (thanks to his father-in-law) he secured a job in a distillery in Dublin.

He would later take over that business and become a monument in Irish whiskey history himself.

John Jameson was a shrewd businessman and highly professional distiller, but he was also an exemplary family man, and a man with a heart of gold. He and Margaret had sixteen children, ten of whom survived their childhood. Four of his sons stayed in the whiskey world, either starting their own distillery or collaborating with others.

He also took great interest in his staff and suppliers. Farmers who could supply him with the best barley were already paid when sowing the grains. His employees were paid twice as much as the normal wage scale. But only under certain conditions. He did not want them to smoke tobacco. They had to get married and father at least two children. After that, he helped the family and children if they had health problems, and with education. But most importantly: every staff member had to promise to drink moderately or to drink no alcohol at all.

John Jameson died on December 3, 1823.

By then the Scottish Jameson family had become the leading whiskey family in Ireland.

56

VON LIEBIG VERSUS PASTEUR

THE SECRET OF FERMENTING

Take two leading chemists, preferably a German and a Frenchman, active in the middle of the nineteenth century. Both should be specialists in the same field. Let's say fermentation, for example. Make sure they come to conflicting conclusions. Allow them to publish their findings, in which both of them show that the other is wrong.

Increase the tension between the two scholars and invite them to get together. In addition, make sure that one of them will decline the invitation. Finally, have a third examiner show that both of them were wrong.

Then you have a scenario for the famous Liebig-Pasteur dispute.

Main characters: the German Justus von Liebig (1803-1873), the man who made stock cubes and discovered chloroform, and the Frenchman Louis Pasteur (1822-1895), from whom we know pasteurisation, among other things.

Von Liebig claimed that fermentation was the result of an absolute chemical process.

He said that yeast wasn't needed at all. The chemical conversion, he contested, was caused by the vibrations in the liquid. Pasteur, on the other hand, insisted that it was only possible because of the microorganisms that got into the mixture. He even believed that oxygen was not needed.

That was the straw that broke the camel's back.

In 1856, Pasteur was attacked by von Liebig in a quarrel that would never be resolved.

But we, whisky lovers, owe a lot to both men.

Researchers in multiple countries have tried to get to the bottom of the squabbles. Forty years later, the German (later Nobel Prize winner) Eduard Buchner and the Japanese Jokichi Takamine, among others, had unravelled most of the secrets of fermentation.

We still use that knowledge to this day.

Fermentation is a very important part of distillation. It's more than releasing a bunch of fungi on a tub of sugar water, hoping that they will feast on the sugars to produce alcohol and other things. It is an accurate interplay of sugars, enzymes, bacteria, and fungi, dancing on the tightrope of temperature fluctuations, acid levels, alcohol levels, oxygen supply, and time.

Craftsmanship. Always greet it with respect.

57

EXCISEMEN
THE MAN WITH THE SECOND KEY

Excise duties are taxes on everything that is tasty.

They're designed to make people unhappy. Some books claim that it came from the Low Countries. The English word excise is said to have been derived from Middle Dutch. It is actually correct: we do know that this was introduced in the Netherlands, around 1596.

It's typical of excise duties that they always increase. Falling excise taxes are short-term mistakes. Increasing excise taxes, on the other hand, are always well-intentioned: usually the government is 'concerned' about our health or about nature.

The king needed money to go to war and the English introduced excise taxes in 1642. The Scots followed suit the following year. The Board of Excise was created after the two British parliaments united in 1707. All the taxes had to be collected by the Board. Money was not

The famous American agents Izzy Einstein and Moe Smith, examples of the British Excisemen.

the only focus. The main goal was to get rid of illegal distilling and the smuggling of alcohol. Excisemen were sent in to inspect.

In 1707, the excisemen travelled along paths trampled by pack animals, sheep, and smugglers. They were often accompanied by someone familiar with the area.

Excise collection became Britain's highest-risk profession. Whoever was sent into the wilderness (with all those barbarians) was not sure if they would make it. Some excisemen preferred to be accompanied by soldiers. But that was arranged at their own expense.

Nobody dared to travel to the Scottish islands. The large landowners on the islands had to collect the taxes.

In the early 1800s, Malcolm Gillespie, a very conscientious controller, dismantled hundreds of illegal distilleries and intercepted tens of thousands of litres of alcohol. Yet, after 28 years of loyal service, he allowed himself to be bribed. He was convicted and hanged (the last hanging ever in Aberdeen).

At the gallows, just before the executioner could do his job, Malcolm uncovered his torso and, hoping for a bit of respite, pointed out the 42 stab scars left over from his career.

The general ban on home distilling came into effect in 1781. Heavy fines were attached to it. In addition, the population was urged to click: a sum of money was given to whoever could designate an illegal distiller or bring in a part of a boiler. Many Scots used this to make money to replace worn parts from their own illegal distillery.

As centuries ago as it always will be: the introduction of new taxes spawned a new sport of evasion. But that is not easy if you live on an island and do not have neighbouring countries where that tax does not apply. The government intervened.

THE EXCISE ACT

The Excise Act went into effect in 1823. Large fines were imposed on illegal distillers, but the Act also made it possible for distillers to buy a license cheaply, so that they could work in full compliance with the law. There was at least one 'but': each distillery had to provide a house on its own property, for the tax inspector to live in.

Accordingly, each distillery had its own controller in-house. From early in the morning to late in the night, he recorded everything that came in and went out of the distillery. All alcohol automatically disappeared into bonded warehouses until the excise duties were paid.

The spirit safe, wherein the new spirit flowed from the stills, now had a beautiful, heavy padlock. To open it you needed two keys. The manager had the first. The exciseman became 'the man with the second key'.

The exciseman's life later became a lot safer. In some places, they quickly became a notable figure of the village. But that wasn't the case everywhere.

Such a stalker who follows you all day, to see what you do and don't do, doesn't necessarily become your best friend so easily.

But the system worked. The government was aware that the money was coming in. On the other hand, the salaries of more than 150 inspectors in Scotland weighed heavily on the total budget. Many governments were delighted to discover a completely new method after the introduction of VAT in 1973: letting one national collect the taxes from another national. The national-collector must then transfer the money to you and, if necessary, advance it himself if the other national did not pay promptly.

Brilliant, you don't have to do anything yourself, and you have everything under control with a few inspectors.

Wasn't there a better way to control the distilleries?

THE RAYNAR REPORT

In 1983 the British government fully understood the problem: they published the Raynar Report, containing an extensive list of 'distillery instructions'. The excisemen were recalled home immediately.

They were done with keeping a close eye on the distillers. From then on, everyone had to be self-controlled.

Exciseman became even more of a risky profession: They were out of a job (luckily there was still VAT and a few otherwise unexplained taxes to be collected). Distillers rejoiced: at last they were rid of those snoopers. But not for long.

After reading the Raynar Report more carefully, they discovered what they were supposed to do.

Everything, just everything. They had to keep track of what was happening in the distillery, neatly pour that info into reports, and send everything to big brother. Every step of the production process had to be recorded: from bringing in the first grain of barley to collecting the last drop of the new spirit. They had to submit a report per week, month, and quarter.

The allowed margin of error on the total production in each of those periods was so small that it is not possible to get you drunk with it.

But that beautiful, antique padlock still hangs on the spirit safe. Sealed. Even if the 'man with the second key' is no longer there. The manager now has control and is responsible for the end result. He pays the fines and is subjected to potentially long prison sentences if there is any suspected fraud.

SMELLERS MUST ENSURE
ALL CASKS ARE SWEET

58

MAILLARD REACTION
DELICIOUS BUT MYSTERIOUS

Just imagine: you return home after a tiring day at work, and your partner has just baked a delicious loaf of bread. The smell of freshly baked bread is something you will never forget. Now you can say anything you want. You compliment the person on their cooking, you might point out that everything is neat, and you may show that you noticed that there is a new bouquet of flowers..

You can come up with any compliment. But beware: never say that this wonderful aroma that lingers in the house after baking did not have anything to do with your partner's culinary arts but that it is the result of the Maillard reaction.

Trust me, you're not going to score with that. On the contrary.

Who's Maillard? What did he do, and what did he have to do with whisky?

Louis Camille Maillard (1878-1936) was a French physician and chemist mainly focused on research of the kidneys, and who broke new ground with his research into food preparation. He was able to understand what happens when you baked, deep-fried, roasted, grilled, or heated a nutrient under certain conditions.

Around 1912, Maillard published his findings on the complicated chemical reaction (or chain of reactions) that would bear his name.

It looks simple. The Maillard reaction is an almost endless chain of chemical reactions between reducing sugars and amino acids (such as proteins), creating brown colours and an incomprehensible bouquet of delicious smells and flavours. Just by heating.

It's a very complex chemical process, depending on temperature, duration of the heating, and the degree of acidity and humidity. Hundreds of flavour components are constantly being created, which then break down and combine to form new flavour components. It is an almost endless series of delicious explosions.

We usually don't think about it. Remember the last time, when you baked that thick ribeye in that delicious butter in that hot pan? That smell? OMG!

You can't take credit. No. Maillard came to visit you.

When it comes to whisky, Maillard comes into play during the malting and drying of the barley. The 'green malt' (the still moist, germinated barley) must be dried to stop further germination. Drying can take place over fires or in drums; and of course, this is always accompanied by high temperatures.

The grains undergo a 'ribeye treatment'.

In beer, you will find the Maillard effect more clearly later in the production, when the colour and taste of the beer are created.

Of course, the flavours of the whiskies will be dominated by the smoke if a lot of peat is used during drying. But even though I know that 60 to 70 percent of the taste and smell of my whisky developed in the cask, I still try to discover where my good friend Louis Camille Maillard has put his signature.

59

THE MAKER'S MARK CASE

YOU SPOKE. WE LISTENED!

Whisky lovers are delicate souls. When a country is hit by strikes, they grumble. They say 'it is always the same' and hope that it passes soon. If a train has an average delay of fifteen minutes, they shake their heads compassionately and wait. But change their favourite drink a bit and they are willing to erect barricades until the calamity is over.

Take a simple incident as an example: from tomorrow, a distiller will no longer bottle his whisky at 45% ABV, but at 42% ABV. Who cares about three percent? Nobody, right? Forget it.

Maker's Mark distillery.

Maker's Mark has been on the market for more than 50 years. The spiritual father of this popular straight bourbon was Bill Samuels Sr., who bought the historic (and now listed) Burks' Distillery in Loretto, Kentucky. Today, Burks belongs to beverage producer Beam Suntory. The Maker's Mark whiskies mature for between five and seven years in new charred barrels and are renowned for their full-bodied taste and verdant followers. In recent decades, their turnover has grown by almost ten percent per year. For a small-batch distillery, this is difficult to keep up.

That's why Rob Samuels, the current chief operating officer and grandson of the founder, decided to reduce the alcohol content in the bottle from 45 to 42% ABV. That way, he could fill more bottles. He did not act overnight. In advance, he subjected a trained panel to a series of blind tastings. It was shown that the old and new versions were imperceptible. Especially if you throw a cube of ice in it, as most Americans do.

He actually had plenty of options. He could have just lowered the ABV and kept it secret. This happened frequently (and perhaps still happens) in the whiskey world. Or to not lower the ABV, but raise the price. Or to allow the whiskey to mature a little bit less.

But no. Honesty is the best policy, thought Rob, and on February 9, 2013, he emailed newspapers, magazines, shops, and fans to announce that Maker's Mark would only be available at 42% ABV.

Immediately afterwards, there was a storm of protest. Even leading magazines like Time Magazine and tabloid newspapers like The Daily Telegraph jumped on it. But the big mudslide came via Twitter and 'social media'.

Whisky clubs organised emergency tastings to compare the two expressions. Whisky blogs got in each other's way to get their comments on the internet first.

Maker's Mark was the talk of the day.

On February 17, Rob Samuels sent another email: 'You spoke. We listened! We never meant to ruin your whiskey. We just wanted to make sure everyone could get a bottle. We'll be sticking to 45% ABV from now on.'

This was a good lesson for the entire whiskey industry, suddenly discovering what it had always neglected: the power of social media. Even the multinational Diageo, known for its strict rules, is now slowly moving away from their 'no picture taking in the distillery' rule (always hated by whiskey lovers).

Every smartphone pic taken by inspired visitors in the distillery can be posted within seconds to Instagram, Twitter, Facebook and other (a)social media platforms. Free, pro bono publicity.

And Maker's Mark?

The distillery couldn't ask for better publicity. And that 45% ABV is still going strong. Anyone who was able to buy a bottle at 42% ABV and leave the plug in it is a very good investor.

60

AH, THOSE SCOTS!

NEVER SATISFIED

You won't hear a negative word about the European Parliament from us. We aren't regulars there and don't know much about it, but they have already managed to get a few things done. For example, the opening in all mailboxes in Europe must be at least 23 centimetres wide. We believe that is just thinking broadly. But even better was the publication of the famous Regulation 110 of 2008: a huge relief for the entire beverage industry.

A Regulation is a set of rules that is sent by 'Europe' to all member states. Those states have to apply those rules to national law within a certain period of time.

Regulation 110 of 15 January 2008 concerns 'the definition, description, presentation, labelling and the protection of geographical indications of spirit drinks'. The regulation provides a detailed definition for 46 drinks so we know exactly what is in a bottle in Europe if it contains the word whisky.

A summary of the regulations might read as follows: whisky is a drink distilled from a mash of malted grains, with or without unmalted cereals. The sacchariffication of the starch must be controlled by the enzymes present, with or without other natural enzymes. The fermentation will be with yeast and the distillation will be no higher than 94.8% ABV. The distillate must then mature for at least three years in wooden barrels no larger than seven hundred litres. When bottling, only water may be added and possibly the colouring agent, caramel. Bottling must be at least at forty percent ABV. And finally, nothing should be added, at any time, that could affect taste or aroma.

Any healthy whisky lover can live with that definition. Did you also think so? But, like me, you did not take the Scots into account.

MORE AND BETTER

On November 23, 2009, Scotland's famous 2009 Directive N° 2890 came into effect. The Scotch Whisky Association (SWA) had scrutinised the European Regulation 110 and 'refined' it. Result: The Scotch Whisky Regulations 2009, which apply to the entire United Kingdom.

They wanted to secure the term 'Scotch whisky' so that other countries were prohibited from using the word 'Scotch' on their bottles. But also, to indicate that the whisky from Scotland met even stricter requirements.

They immediately deleted the phrase 'with or without other natural enzymes' from the European definition. Consequently, for Scotch whisky, only the enzymes from the grains themselves are used.

That doesn't make it any easier. On the contrary. Identical enzymes, developed in laboratories, require much less control and fine-tuning in terms of temperature and acidity during the saccharification of the starch. Without those other nature-identical enzymes, more craftsmanship emerges. According to the Scots, their whiskies are a step up.

Europe speaks of 'wooden barrels', but the Scots stick to 'oak barrels'. You are accordingly not allowed to experiment with other types of wood, such as chestnut or beech. In other countries, most distilleries tend to stick to oak as well, as tests show that other woods

Coopers can be recognised by their tattoos.

give worse results. But nothing prevents them from using a barrel made from, for example, hazel wood.

Only when all the rules of Europe and also those of Scotland have been met, can the label of the bottle say 'SCOTCH WHISKY'.

But there is more: in Scotland no whisky other than Scotch whisky may be produced. So, there is no other Scotch whisky than *'Scotch whisky'*.

A smart Scot who thinks: 'I don't need a "Scotch" on my label, so I only stick to the European rules' can forget it.

When you can buy a bottle that only states 'Whisky made in Scotland', you have to think twice.

61

TOWSER AND SHORTIE
HARDWORKING FOUR-LEGGED FRIENDS

In the past, it used to be different. You couldn't enter a distillery without cats walking right in front of you. They were a part of the workforce. Their names were almost always whisky-related, like Peaty, Smokey, Amber, Yeast, and Barley. Their job was to keep the granaries free of mice.

But times are changing. In most distilleries, malting isn't carried out in-house anymore. Accordingly the grain lofts are empty. And to make matters worse for cats, new editions appeared of both the Health and Safety at Work Regulations and the Modern Food Hygiene Regulations.

Cats, among others, became victims. They were suddenly a danger to our health. The regulations stated: 'Breach of the regulations is a crime throughout the UK'. Every 'felis silvestris domesticus' in every distillery lost its job. But some cats persist, such as the one at Bladnoch Distillery. On my last visit, it just sat next to the visitor centre's cash register and showed its claws every time the drawer opened.

Luckily Towser, the legendary female cat at the Glenturret Distillery, didn't have to go through this. The little sweetheart died in 1984, after 24 years of faithful service. But contrary to the case for most cats, her name is chiselled into a wall there, and it appears in Guinness World Records.

Born on April 21, 1963, Towser, a long-haired tortoiseshell cat with red-black fur, is said to have caught no fewer than 28,899 mice in her career at Glenturret. I know, you'll ask me: 'Who counted that?' I was told that two sworn bailiffs followed the cat uninterrupted for a fortnight. Based on the result of their count, they extrapolated the total. Towser was rightly given a bronze statue in the distillery.

↓ Towser immortalised.

And there's more! If you're lucky, you may find a bottle of Fairlie's Light Highland liqueur in some liquor stores. It's a fairly rare bottle, which you won't be able to pick up for less than two hundred pounds. The secret? The delicious whisky liqueur, but also the fact that the bottle bears 'imprints' of Towser's paw (considerably reduced in size).

And then there was Shortie. Shortie was not a cat, but a Jack Russell Terrier. He was also not on the pay list of the Ardbeg distillery, where he felt at home. He was the neighbour's dog. But, punctually every day, he waited until the door of the distillery was opened for him. Shortie could be found everywhere in the distillery, even in places where the common visitor was kept out. In the evening, he would return home satisfied.

One thing is certain: Shortie can never be accused of having harmed a single mouse or other vermin.

The dog was everyone's friend and is known even in the farthest corners of Asia.

With Shortie gone, Ardbeg uses his name and image for one of their whiskies.

Dare to touch those bottles.

In March 2020, the distillery launched its first beer: THE SHORTIE, a smoked porter. The proceeds go to a drinking water project in Africa.

We sympathise with the distilleries who lost a beautiful marketing tool when cats and dogs left.

If that was ever the purpose of the Health and Safety Regulations (which we doubt very much) they may have overlooked something: the Arran distillery, on the Scottish island of the same name, boasts a couple of 'golden eagles' which regularly fly graceful circles high above the mountains during visiting hours. During the construction of the distillery, building was stopped for several weeks after learning that the golden eagles were breeding.

62

SHAKEN OR STIRRED?

ASK JAMES

Let's take a look at all the scenes in which the legendary James Bond ordered his vodka martini 'shaken not stirred'.

Decor: a lavish bar with suspicious looking patrons. Enters: Bond in full uniform, unsuspecting. There is only one free seat at the bar, next to a beautiful (Russian) black-haired goddess, with eyes like a doe, and a dress so narrow that no one could suspect even the smallest item is hidden underneath. Except for James, who has long noticed that a Smith & Wesson 617 calibre 22 is concealed under her garter.

What is James doing in this case? He orders a vodka martini, 'shaken not stirred'. Knowing his trade, the bartender serves him a perfect vodka martini, shaken not stirred. James happily takes one sip, then gets a massive blow to the back of the head with a blackjack that the Russian happened to have in her handbag. The next morning, James wakes up in Kathmandu.

And now for the worst part: nobody will ever wonder what happened to his vodka martini.

Was it worth it for only one sip, not to 'stir', but to 'shake'? And does that also apply to whisky?

We searched theses to see if specialists knew what the difference was. Professor Metin Tolan of the University of Dortmund puts it simply: 'If you just stir your drink, you distribute all the molecules evenly in the glass. When you start "shaking", you bring up the tastiest molecules. The first sip you take will therefore contain the tastiest parts of your drink.' A shaken vodka martini would also contain more antioxidants than a stirred one, he claims.

Although I'd wager that James didn't know that last fact, the former proves that James Bond is a genius: the first sip is the best. In no episode does he get the chance to take a second sip. That's why 'shaken not stirred' is James' lifelong slogan.

Still.

The expression 'shaken not stirred' was not originally used by James Bond in Ian Fleming's books, but was used by his nemesis Dr No. Accordingly, James stole it from him.

But what about whisky? Jim McEwan, the legendary master distiller, has the habit of shaking a bottle of whisky in his masterclasses to show whether the whisky contains less or more than 46% ABV alcohol. If the alcohol percentage is 46% or higher, you will get bubbles on the surface. If it is lower, no bubbles.

Should you shake your whisky in your glass? Or stir? Let it roll around? Heat it up? Add water to it?

Keep calm. Never forget: it's your whisky. You decide.

TONGUE TWISTERS
GAELIC FOR BEGINNERS

In 2017 a brand-new distillery opened on the Scottish peninsula of Morvern, opposite the Isle of Mull. You can visit the distillery, although it is not easy. If we can give you some good advice: take the boat.

There is a weekly water taxi from Tobermory and a regular car ferry from Fishnish, to Lochaline.

Otherwise, you have only one option: you take the Corran ferry at Ballachulish and then drive towards Strontian. Should you meet anyone along the way, which is to some extent doubtful, just ask about the Nc'nean Distillery, the most remote distillery in Scotland.

How do you pronounce its name? Oh, simple: nook-knee-anne, with the emphasis on 'knee'.

That's what I like about the names of many Scotch whisky distilleries. They are true tongue twisters. But we are here to help you.

Scottish Gaelic is the source of the most difficult distillery names. Gaelic is an impossible language with far too few letters. It has only five vowels and thirteen consonants, of which the 'h' is only used to form some sounds with other letters and thus form letters that the language does not know: the j, k, q, v, w, x, y and z. But there is even more to watch out for: you don't always have to pronounce all the letters in a word. On the other hand, you sometimes have to pronounce letters that are not there. Can you follow? An example: Scotland is 'Alba' in Scottish Gaelic. Pronounced 'a-la-ba'. Also: 'aoi' is pronounced like 'uhyee', 'bh' and 'mh' sound like 'v', 'pf' is 'f', and 'gh' or 'dh' resemble 'y'. The emphasis is usually on the second syllable, but sometimes also on the third.

So, now you know enough. Here we go: Allt-a-Bhainne (alt a vain); Ardnamurchan (ard ne Muur ken); Glen Garioch (glen gierie); Bruichladdich (brook lad die); Bunnahabhain (boe nah hav en); Glenallachie (glen alla kie); Knockando (nok an doo); and Strathisla (strait aai la). And this is a difficult one: Auchroisk is 'ar trusk'.

When the Auchroisk distillery launched its first bottles in 1986, the manager decided not to put 'Auchroisk' on the label. Instead, he went for 'Singleton'. This way, he was sure that nobody would have any problems ordering the right bottle. In 2001, the multinational beverage company Diageo changed its name back to Auchroisk. The whisky has become such a success that no matter how you pronounced the name, everyone understood you meant an 'ar trusk'.

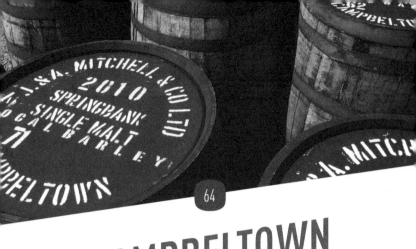

CAMPBELTOWN
WHISKY CAPITAL OF THE WORLD

When Thomas Pennant, a naturalist and avid traveller from Wales, made his way through Scotland in 1772, at the time a perilous undertaking, he ended up in Campbeltown in the south of the Kintyre peninsula. In his travelogue he always gave a lot of details, but he rarely mentioned whisky.

What he discovered in Campbeltown was a little too much for him.

'Although there is normally enough barley, the stock now regularly turns out to be insufficient,' he wrote. 'However, the inhabitants are stupid enough to turn their barley into a poisonous drink. Every year they burn hundreds of kilos of barley in what they call whisky. That turns out to be the modern drink. They used to make it from thyme, mint, anise and some other herbs. They called it "usquebaugh" and drank it very moderately. But now! The Duke of Argyle, the main owner of this area, goes to great lengths to discourage this harmful practice, but the trade is so profitable that the entire business is now geared to it. The women used to work the flax that grew here, but now it is the men that have to work in the fields, while the women distill whisky at home. Yes, all those "modern" drinks. All that distilling in Campbeltown and the surroundings is illegal, of course. But if the legislator ever would get involved and would introduce licenses, this could be a sound basis for broad production.'

A HUNDRED YEARS LATER

When Alfred Barnard visited Campbeltown's licensed distilleries in 1878 for his famous book 'The Whisky Distilleries of the United Kingdom', 21 distilleries appeared on his list. Campbeltown, then already known as 'the whisky capital of the world', at its peak had 26 hard-working distilleries in a town of about 9,000 inhabitants. There had been more distilleries previously, but some had already stopped. The 'wee town', as the locals call Campbeltown, holds about five thousand inhabitants today. The decline of the whisky industry in the last centuries hurt the town badly.

In 1998 only two distilleries remained: Springbank and Glen Scotia. The Scotch Whisky Association (SWA) decided to no longer consider Campbeltown a 'protected region'.

It was a kick in the teeth to Hedley Wright, the owner of Springbank.

From then on, anyone could put 'Campbeltown Whisky' on their label, no matter where that whisky was distilled.

'If Lowlands with (at that time) only three distilleries could get a 'protected region' label, why not Campbeltown with two distilleries?' reasoned Wright.

Wright would be one step ahead of the SWA. He bought the buildings of the Glengyle Distillery, which closed in 1925, a stone's throw from Springbank, and completely renovated it. That way, in 2004 a third distillery in Campbeltown came into being. The Scotch Whiskey Association surrendered and 'Campbeltown Whisky' again became an appellation d'origine contrôlé.

In the Scotch Whisky Regulations, which first appeared in 2009, everything was laid out again.

The Lost Lochruan Distillery in Campbeltown.

Scotland has three **Protected Regions**: the Lowlands, the Highlands, and Speyside. The border between the Highlands and the Lowlands is the famous Highland Line (see above). Speyside is a well-defined area around the River Spey. As the Speyside region is in the middle of the Highlands, Speyside distilleries are allowed to choose which of the two denominations - Highlands or Speyside - they list on the label.

In addition, Scotland has two **Protected Locations**: Islay and Campbeltown. Those names may only appear on the bottle if all the whisky in that bottle has been distilled at those locations.

But that applies to every place name that is mentioned on a label, protected location or not.

If a label states 'Orkney Single Malt Scotch Whisky', you can be sure that the whisky is distilled on Orkney, at least if the five words are on the bottle in exactly that order. That mandatory order is also stated in the Regulations.

Nitpickers, those Scots? Forget it, they place the dots where they belong and that pays off. Even internationally.

In 2019, the SWA campaigned successfully to have the American Virginia Distillery Company remove the 'Highland whisky' designation from its labels. During the same period, the government of Cambodia, at the urging of the SWA, decided that no designations referring to Scotland may be used on their spirits.

65

ZERO POINT ZERO ZERO ZERO ZERO...

CARAMEL AND WHISKY

European and Scottish legislation is clear: before whisky is bottled, only water and/or the colorant caramel may be added. The latter divides the whisky world into two camps: those who have no problem with it and those who shudder at the thought alone. Among the opponents you will even find 'experts' who claim to be able to taste whether there is caramel in it or not. According to them, it should be mandatory to indicate on the label whether the whisky has been coloured. Today this is the case in Germany and Denmark.

What is a colorant exactly? How much do you need to get a result? The effect is simple: the addition makes the whisky a tad darker, and the buyer could easily make the link between 'dark whisky' and 'aged whisky' and between 'old' and 'better'. Consequently, it might be seen to promote sales. That may be true, but why then do they put the bottle in a tube or box afterwards. You can't even see the colour.

A more logical explanation could be that with each new batch of malt whisky there may be a slight colour difference compared to the previous one. Regular customers find it annoying that one single malt is light amber with a gold rim, but the next isn't.

What is caramel? If you heat sugar long enough and in a controlled manner, the sugar will turn brown and runny. If you cool it afterwards, you get... candies. If you heat sugar and add certain chemicals, such as ammonia or sulphite, you get a completely different reaction.

This creates several dark dyes that scientists have conveniently called E150a, E150b, E150c and E150d. They all have different characteristics and, therefore, different applications. E150d, for example, is used in cola (and could be unhealthy were you to drink a thousand glasses a day). The E150c can be found in several beers and E150b can be found in cognac. Only E150a is used for whisky.

So how much should you add? To find out more, we visited Pedro Saez del Burgo, master distiller and master blender. 'The problem is, no law says exactly how much can be used,' said Pedro. 'And, it must not be mentioned on the bottle. But I can assure you that if caramel is used, it will be very little: 0.00004% is acceptable. On the other hand, caramel is difficult to dose. There is no such thing as a 'drop' of caramel, the liquid is much too thick for that. First you have to dilute the substance to a thousandth, for example, to make it somewhat measurable. 0.00004 % means four centilitres per hundred thousand litres. If someone tells you he can taste it, just ask if it was good. Caramel is very bitter.'

Okay, all this caramel fuss is nothing more than a storm in a glass... of whisky.

66

HOLY WATER
THREE DROPS IS ENOUGH

Four hundred litres of water is required to distil a litre of alcohol. At each step of the production process, you have to either add water, or extract water, or use water to heat, or use water to cool down.

Fortunately, a lot of those four hundred litres can be recycled.

Nevertheless, at the very last moment, before the whisky goes into the bottle, some water has to be added to get the alcohol content to the right level. And then we're finished.

Did you really think so?

We did not discuss which water to use! Spring water? River water? Well water? Rainwater? Tap water? Soft water? Hard water? Peat water? Demineralized water? There's been a lot of talk about that. After many years of studies, tests and checks, people have come to the conclusion that the nature of the water actually has less influence on the final result than was thought. Peat water will probably leave a 'ground taste' in the whisky. When saccharifying the starch, mineral-rich water will likely increase the activity of the enzymes, but it is hard to find their input in the final result.

It's nice to know.

But connoisseurs are also telling us: 'If you would like to fully enjoy your whisky, add a few drops of water to your drink!'

Water? My whisky is at 43% ABV, that means 57% of the contents of my bottle is water! Why would I then add three more drops?

The connoisseur will answer: 'Because those drops of water create reactions with the alcohol. The booze starts to heat up a bit, resulting in more evaporation. Accordingly, you get more aroma. Especially, the fruity and floral scents which escape more quickly.'

Just add tap water? No, you idiot!

The best water is the same spring water that is used in distillation. You can indeed buy that water in some distilleries. It costs almost as much as the whisky itself. There is only one solution in the absence of that spring water: the water you have at hand, non-sparkling bottled water, or tap water.

Or... No... A better idea. Wait.

Go to Scotland, go to Aberlour.

It takes some searching to find it, but the first Scotsman you meet will show you the way to Saint Drostan's Well, an ancient well. Saint Drostan was a follower of the legendary Saint Columba in the seventh century. He baptised many of those wild Caledonians in this very same spring. The water turned out to have a very particular power: after drinking, a blind man could see again; a cripple could walk again. You've heard the stories before.

Therefore, if you put this spring water in your whisky: guys, guys...

Well, there is only one distillery that works with this spring water: Aberlour Distillery.

Sparkling water.

It is, to my knowledge, the only distillery that uses 'holy' water. Remember that name, because the whisky is quite good (one of the six best-selling Scotch whiskies). I haven't had that whisky very often and so I can't give you more details about the effect of the water on my eyes and bones. But it's worth a try.

Most of the Scotch whiskies are bottled near Glasgow and Edinburgh. Let's follow a whisky, distilled on Islay, brought to Glasgow in tankers, barrelled in Glasgow and left there for fifteen years to mature.

Do you think they will bring over another set of tankers containing water from the same well on Islay to add to the spirit before bottling?

Or do they use local water?

An inexhaustible supply of peat on Islay.

67

HIDE A CASE

PLAYING HIDE AND SEEK

Canadian Club, better known as 'CC' by connoisseurs, is a Canadian rye whisky with American roots. In 1858, Hiram Walker of Detroit, a vinegar maker, had the idea of switching to whisky. He was right: whisky tastes better than vinegar. He acquired land near Windsor, Ontario, in Canada, where he founded his distillery. His top product, Hiram Walker's Club Whisky, quickly became a great success, not just in Canada, but also in the United States.

The American distillers did not like this. They asked the US government to protect their own whiskies and demanded that all 'Canadian whisky' bottles should bear the word Canada. The demand was approved. Walker changed the name of his whisky to Canadian Club. It became, and still is, one of the four most sold whiskies in the United States. Canadian Club would go on to become a favourite of Queen Elisabeth II. Today Canadian Club is owned by Beam Suntory.

In 1967, a marketer of the distillery came up with a brilliant idea that would become one of the largest and longest-running promotions in whisky history: 'Hide a Crate'.

It was as simple as a promotion should be: hide a crate with twelve bottles of whisky somewhere in an impossible place, give hints in your ads about where to find them, and let people search. Whoever finds a box can keep it, and they'll also receive an extra prize. They didn't run the promotion with just one crate, but twenty-five. They were hidden all over the world between 1967 to 1991.

There was one on Mount Kilimanjaro in Tanzania. The crate was quickly located. A second was hidden behind the highest waterfall in the world: Angel Falls in Venezuela (discovered after seven months by a honeymoon couple). Fishermen found a crate in the Great Barrier Reef, Australia, eleven years after it was dropped there. Someone found a box in Death Valley, California. Even an abandoned gold mine was not a safe place to hide bottles. Another box was discovered underneath a Manhattan office unit.

Sixteen crates have since been found. There are nine more to be found. Nobody in the company knows where three of these are.

To help you... some hints: Loch Ness in Scotland, Robinson Crusoe Island near Chile, Yukon Territory in Canada, at the North Pole, somewhere around Lake Placid in New York, and thirty meters from where Stanley and Livingston met in Ujiji, Tanzania.

Now you know enough, what are you waiting for?

Although I also have to disappoint you: that extra super prize is no longer there. In 2010 they tried to revive the action. However, they turned it into an impossibly complicated matter, with puzzles and questions and assignments. Even an extra price of one hundred thousand dollars could not help to save the campaign. Interest in the game faded, and the company decided to end it.

But don't be discouraged: the bottles are still there and if you ever find a crate, here's our advice: every box contains twelve bottles, worth a lot as a collector's item. Drink eleven and your twelfth bottle is worth a fortune.

This is the KISS principle that the Canadian Club marketers unfortunately renounced in 2010: 'Keep it Simple, Keep it Stupid.'

68

TENNESSEE WHISKEY

THE LINCOLN COUNTY PROCESS

Let's break down the title: 'process' refers to a method used in whiskey production in the US.

'Lincoln County' is a reference to the 'province' where the method is supposed to have originated.

But, there are 23 counties in the US called Lincoln County.

There is actually a Lincoln County in Tennessee, but it is not the Lincoln County where the method would have originated. The Lincoln County we are looking for doesn't exist anymore. Because, after Prohibition, many counties were changed.

Clear, isn't it?

It doesn't matter, because the method had been used several centuries before by every experienced illegal distiller, in all corners of the United States. It was used long before Jack Daniel revived the process, in 1866, at his distillery in Lincoln County, Tennessee. Due to the redrawing of the boundaries, the distillery is now located in Moone County.

The process can be summarized as follows: when the new spirit has been distilled, the distiller drips the liquid through a column of charcoal, three to four metres high, and afterwards through a thick woollen blanket.

This action usually lasts several days, sometimes a whole week. It happens before the new spirit enters the barrel.

The production of the charcoal is carried out with sugar maple wood, a hard type of wood, which is also often used for bowling alleys. Large mounds of cross-stacked slats are set on fire and kept wet to create the charcoal.

The result of the process is astonishing: a sweet, smooth, mild whiskey is created by the filtering. In 1941, the US government decided that this whiskey could be called 'Tennessee Whiskey' if it was made using this method in Tennessee.

In 2013, a new law required all whiskey in Tennessee to be produced that way.

But there are only two distilleries in this state: Jack Daniel and George Dickel.

The first uses the word 'whiskey', the other 'whisky'.

69

BOTTLE DECOMPOSITION

NICE LITTLE FRAGMENT

There it is! Finally. In front of you on the table. How long did it take for you to make that decision? Yes, understandably, you don't buy a whisky with such a high price every day.

But now is the time to act! Finally, you can open the bottle. You will be able to smell that glorious aroma. Then you will take that first sip, a few drops on your tongue. Your mouth is filled with an endless collection of wonderful flavours. And after enjoying it for a while, you get a great, complex and long finish... Waaw!

But wait, let's take a closer look at that bottle first. Not the colour of the liquid, but the label. It is clearly marked there: 58% ABV! That means: 58% of the content of your bottle is pure alcohol. And I have to disappoint you: pure alcohol is colourless, odourless and tasteless. It's just what it is: alcohol.

CONGENERS
WATER

ETHANOL

🜄 Make no mistake: not all the alcohol is at the bottom.

No fear, there's still 42% of your bottle left. It's not mentioned on the label, but it's easy to figure out: this part of your bottle is... water. Pure water. And honestly: pure water too is colourless, odourless and tasteless. It is just what it is: water.

How much did you pay for that bottle? OMG!

No, wait, what I was saying above is not correct! The water in the bottle is not 42% of the total, but only 41.8% (approximately). There is still 0.2% to investigate.

A good thing, too! These are the congeners. Most of the smell and taste of your whisky can be attributed to them. They are esters, aldehydes, tannins, acids, methanol, heavier alcohols and other chemicals, which are mainly formed during fermentation and maturation.

Fortunately, you do not get all the congeners that distilling entails. Some are harmful and, accordingly, should be avoided as much as possible. It is the master distiller's job to know exactly which part of his output he will keep and put into the barrels.

The job isn't finished. In each barrel there will be an interplay between the wood, the air and the new spirit. An interplay that will last for years and creates new flavours.

We pay a hefty price for only 0.2%.

THE BATTLE OF THE CROWS

NOT EVERY CROW IS AN OLD CROW

Around 1950, Gaines Company, the producer of the legendary Old Crow Whiskey, advertised in several American newspapers:

'In the last fifty years of our existence, we have dealt with over 1,800 subpoenas, lawsuits, complaints and disclaimers... Simply to challenge the many thefts of our Old Crow brand name.'

It was the longest judicial dispute in the world of whiskey.

It all began with the Scotsman James C. Crow, born in Inverness in 1789. He graduated from the University of Edinburgh with a degree in medicine and chemistry. The man became a good doctor, but he felt that Scotland was too small for him.

He and his brother went to America in 1823. He started a small business but it ended badly. He looked for new opportunities in Frankfort, Kentucky, where he came in contact with Colonel Field, the proprietor of a small distillery.

When they decided to work together, James was given the opportunity to apply the knowledge he had brought from Scotland.

He was the first distiller to do real scientific work to improve the whiskey produced.

He is often referred to as 'the father of the sour mash', but some experts disagree with this.

Sour mash is a way of fermenting that is typical for bourbon whiskey. It works like sourdough in bread baking: part of the previous fermentation is added to the new fermentation to activate it.

James carefully controlled every step in the process.

He brought out his many instruments (and his litmus paper strips) to accurately measure the sugar content of the mixture, the acidity, etc. This allowed him to adjust where necessary, and make a better whiskey.

He moved to the Old Oscar Pepper Distillery, where he created his unique whiskey, Old Crow. The whiskeys were fought over. Everyone wanted his Old Crow: presidents, congressmen, artists, actors, writers. Mark Twain was a supporter. The presidents Grant and Lincoln loved Old Crow.

The beginning of the end of Old Crow was marked by the death of James Crow in 1856. There was still a lot of stock in the maturation warehouses, and it was hard to find the whiskey on the market.

It made the bottles even more attractive to the buyer. Old Crow became a widely sought-after whiskey.

A former colleague of James Crow, who worked with him at the Old Oscar Pepper Distillery, joined de Gaines, Berry & Company.

He knew enough to recreate a 'kind' of Old Crow.

Gaines patented his look-alike Crow.

Twenty years after James' death, it wasn't possible to get your hands on a 'real' Old Crow. Jim Beam took over what was left of the Gaines, Berry & Co business in 1987. They kept the name 'Old Crow' on the labels, but filled the bottles with their own bourbon.

THE HELLMANS

In 1840 two children, Isaac and Louis Hellman, emigrated from Bavaria to America. They were seven and ten years old. Thirty years later, we find them in St. Louis, running a liquor store. They bought large quantities of whiskey, mixed it into the most diverse blends and marketed a dozen different brands.

One of those blends got the proud name Crow, another was called Old Crow. But the Hellmans did not patent the brand names.

Both Crows sold well and, in 1907, the brand name was triumphantly elongated to 'Hellman's Celebrated Old Crow', each bottle neatly wrapped in paper.

That's the legendary straw that broke the camel's back: Gaines Company went to the federal court and lost the lawsuit.

The Hellmans had described Gaines' Crow as poisonous and dangerous to public health and on the market for a shorter time than their Crow. The judges, probably not drinkers, believed them. But Gaines didn't stop there. A cascade of lawsuits followed.

Until 1918. The Hellman Distilling Company was convicted by the United States Supreme Court for misusing a trademark and violating the rights of another company.

The Old Crow was saved, but not for long: in 1920 the famous Eighteenth Amendment came into effect in the US. Prohibition forced distilleries to stop production.

COLLECTOR'S ITEM

You can still buy an Old Crow from the 1960s or 1970s. You may pay between four and five hundred dollars. An Old Crow made by James Crow himself is a real museum piece. You can only dream of it.

How about Hellman's Celebrated Old Crow? The production of that Old Crow stopped as a result of Prohibition. Every bottle that exists was made before 1920. And would be worth a lot.

You have to be very lucky to get one.

Or to find one. Bryan Fyte found a bottle in July of 2012 in St. Joseph, Missouri, when he was renovating the bathroom in his newly purchased house.

71

GAN BEI

AND SEE WHAT HAPPENS

'Gan bei' is a national cry in (among other countries) Taiwan. It means 'ad fundum', simply pouring your drink without hesitation. That is what usually happens when this cry is heard. Particularly by or after meals. Even with a menu of seven courses. Each course has a bottle served with it. Usually that bottle is already empty before the first bite.

Ask for a whisky as an aperitif at a Taiwanese restaurant and Black Label will be your best bet. There's nothing wrong with that. But you can only get that whisky per bottle. It's difficult to handle when you are alone, but with a few friends, the job is done quickly.

Drinking together is an important part of Taiwanese culture. The word drinking is related to 'poetry, party, and singing'. You are excluded if you aren't drinking with the group.

Sixty percent of Taiwanese people maintain that they only drink during the weekends, yet alcohol consumption is increasing every year. Do the Taiwanese have it so easy with booze? Better than people from the western world? Forget it.

It's not hard for any of us to take a few whiskies.

The question is what your body does with it.

Alcohol has to be broken down by our body. That takes time, requiring water and enzymes. The necessary enzymes are produced by our body, but we have to supply sufficient water ourselves. Unfortunately, we don't have 'time' under control.

There are several steps in the breakdown of alcohol.

> Step 1: The enzyme alcohol dehydrogenase (ADH) converts the alcohol into ethanal.
> Step 2: The enzyme aldehyde dehydrogenase (ALDH) converts the ethanal into acetic acid.
> Step 3: Acetic acid is further broken down by the body into water and carbon dioxide.

Well, and phew... the case is resolved.

But no: that ethanal (in step 1) is a toxic substance which affects our organs and is the root cause of our suspicious bad breath and (among other things) our hangover the day after. Consequently, it's all about getting that filthy ethanal out of our body as quickly as possible.

And westerners are better equipped for that than our brethren from Southeast Asia. Chinese, Taiwanese, Japanese, and Vietnamese people have much stronger ADH enzymes. Therefore, the production of toxic ethanal is much higher for them. They get drunk quicker because of this. They suffer more from nausea and vomiting, and they have heavy hangovers which last longer.

To make the situation worse, their misery lasts for longer because the ALDH enzyme (in step 2) works weakly.

But from experience, they always remain incredibly hospitable, friendly, and cheerful people.

72

ERNEST SHACKLETON
WHISKY AND ICE

Ernest Shackleton refused to become a doctor even though his father, a doctor himself, desired it. Adventure had already bubbled up in Ernest when he was a teenager. He was very young when he became a cabin boy on a merchant ship. A few years later, he would become a second lieutenant in the Royal Navy. That opened up opportunities for him on far horizons.

In 1901, at the age of 27, Ernest Shackleton joined Robert Scott's Discovery Expedition as a lieutenant, bound for the 'unreachable' South Pole. Shackleton the explorer was born. But it would not go well for him: he had to return early in 1903 because he contracted scurvy on the way.

Antarctica, however, did not let go of him. His own South Pole expedition was set up in the years that followed. He acquired a ship, the Nimrod, and left New Zealand on January 1, 1908.

Ernest Shackleton.

Destination: the McMurdo Islands, where research stations can still be found today.

On February 6, members of the expedition started to build their cabin, at Cape Royds in Antarctica. The cabin would become the shelter for the entire team, the four remaining ponies, and his Arrol-Johnston car (the very first car in Antarctica).

In October, Shackleton left for the South Pole with three of his friends. After 73 difficult days, the explorers had to admit that the coming winter made it impossible to continue.

They were 170 kilometres away from their target.

The only salvation was to return home as soon as possible, hoping that the Nimrod could escape the ice. It worked and, in 1909, Shackleton was back home. And very famous. He was raised to nobility. Since then, he has been referred to as Sir Ernest Shackleton. He became even more famous later for his legendary Endurance Expedition of 1914.

But he will be remembered by whisky lovers for a completely different fact.

MACKINLAY BLENDED MALT

Several explorers visited the cabin after Shackleton's expedition left. According to their stories, it was clear that Shackleton and his team had left in a hurry (there was leftover food from the last meal on the table) and the place was deteriorating.

In 1959, the New Zealand government decided to restore the cabin and secure the entire contents on site. It would take another fifty years for a specialized team to catalogue the contents of the building.

In 2006, they discovered the 'Shackleton's treasure': chests full of bottles, frozen in the Arctic ice. According to some sources, Shackleton had 25 cases of whisky on the Nimrod. We know he was a heavy drinker. The New Zealanders noted that they found five crates of whisky and two crates of brandy in the cabin.

It would take three years before the New Zealand government allowed some bottles to be excavated. They collected several hundred-year-old bottles of 'Mackinlay's Rare Old Highland Malt' (a blended malt) and of 'The Hunter Valley Distillery' (an Australian whisky).

The name Mackinlay is still owned by Whyte & Mackay. Richard 'Goodness Nose' Patterson is the master blender of that same company. It was obvious that he would go after such a bottle.

It took a few years, but he was able to get his hands on three of these bottles. Richard Patterson must have been in heaven when he got to hold that first 'Antarctic wee dram' under his world-famous nose.

The whisky is, of course, carefully dissected. It turned out that the alcohol content in the bottle was 47.3% ABV. That was the correct choice for a dram that had to go to South Pole... or at least 'on the edge'! Because alcohol, just like the water in the bottle, freezes (albeit not so fast: alcohol freezes around -114°C). A mixture of 47.3% ABV then freezes at -114 times 0.473, that is around -54°C. This is about the average temperature at the South Pole. No wonder a lot of bottles were broken. Fortunately, not all.

The analysis also showed that Glen Mhor malt whisky (pronounced 'glen vor') was the main ingredient of the blend. The Glen Mhor Distillery has been closed since 1983. It now houses a department store.

It was one of Inverness's three distilleries. Glen Mhor, together with sister distillery Glen Albyn, used water from Loch Ness for the production, and that must have given it a special touch. The then hard to get single malt was widely praised.

Neil Miller Gunn, the Scottish author, once wrote after drinking a Glen Mhor: 'Until a man has been lucky enough to drink this perfectly aged Glen Mhor, he doesn't know what whisky is.'

73

THE QUEEN AND HER UNITS

14 OR 21 OR 56?

Does Elizabeth II—Queen of the United Kingdom of Great Britain and Northern Ireland, Canada, Australia, New Zealand and a dozen more Commonwealth countries—drink?

We're the last to say that, but it was her ex-chef who inadvertently suggested it.

The Queen reaches for a glass up to four times a day, according to ex-chef Darren McGrady, who has offered faithful service in her kitchen for many years. Before noon, she already has a gin with Dubonnet, wine at lunchtime, another gin and Dubonnet after dinner, and champagne in the evening.

This is 'gefundenes fressen' for the tabloid press in the UK. Doesn't the Queen know that three units a day is the maximum? She is way above that with her licentious behaviour! Shame!

Just as I write this, I have a bottle of Old Pulteney Single Malt in front of me, twelve years old. The label on the back shows a little drawn bottle marked with the words '40 UK UNITS' (I'm in Scotland).

The producer and the government wanted me to know that I should drink from that bottle responsibly.

In January 2016, the Chief Medical Officer in the UK, the person who is officially responsible for the health of all Britons, decided that from then on, everyone should stick to 14 units a week instead of the previously stated 21 units.

The big question, of course, is what is a unit? A unit is the unit measure to indicate the amount of alcohol in an alcoholic beverage. One unit is one centilitre (or eight grams) of pure alcohol.

My Old Pulteney is forty percent ABV, therefore forty units.

The committee of experts decided in 1987 that 21 units per week was the acceptable maximum. The advice was changed because people saved up their daily units for the weekend. Accordingly, the rule was supplemented with 'maximum three to four units per day for men and two or three for women'. That well-intentioned rule of the National Health Service has been met with a lot of criticism.

Newspapers such as *The Guardian* and *The Times* wrote that the numbers were completely out of the blue and that the whole action made no sense. Nevertheless, eighty percent of beverage manufacturers agreed to display 'unit count' on all of their products.

TO THE QUEEN

In 2009, in an Irish pub, I had a long conversation with a man who was completely unknown to me.

He was a doctor who used to be a member of the conscious alcohol committee. We had already tasted a number of whiskies together. He was a connoisseur. Then he told me that the maximum number of units was initially set at 56 per week. Until someone noticed

You can't miss it, on every bottle.

that this was quite a lot. In consultation, the number was reduced to 21. But the registrar mistakenly noted '21 a day', and that was printed on the first leaflets distributed in this campaign. Fortunately, not for long.

But what about my Old Pulteney? At this writing, I have drunk around four centilitres. That's only 1.6 units.

And what about the Queen? After his interview was published, Darren McGrady stated that the journalist had completely misinterpreted him. With the drinks mentioned, he had listed the Queen's favourite drinks and not her daily dose. He admitted that the Queen always wants some whisky in certain sauces.

But does she drink whisky?

Some claim she's not averse to a Johnnie Walker. But Karen Dolby writes in her book 'The Wicked Wit of Queen Elizabeth II' that the Queen only wants spherical ice cubes in her glass. So, it might be true.

BY APPOINTMENT

by Appointment to
Their Majesties The King & Queen
❖❖and to Their late Majesties❖❖
Queen Victoria & King Edward VII

74

ROYAL WHISKY
THE PURVEYORS TO THE ROYAL HOUSEHOLD

Admit it. It would be nice on your letterhead and on all of your products: 'Purveyors to the Royal Household'. Don't put it on your Bentley. It will make people jealous. It isn't a title given out to everybody. It requires either a lot of effort or having a friend at the royal court.

But do you know what's even better? To get permission to use 'ROYAL' in your company name. That's the best! Prefix or suffix, it doesn't matter.

In the whisky world, there are only three lucky ones: Royal Brackla, Royal Lochnagar and Glenury Royal. Unfortunately, the latter disappeared years ago.

We can find the Brackla Distillery near Scotland's Cawdor Castle, southeast of Inverness, where (according to Shakespeare) Macbeth killed his rival Duncan. But Shakespeare did it for the money. He manipulated the story to please his patron, King James VI, because James was a Duncan descendant, so Macbeth had to be the bad guy. 'Fake news'.

Captain William Fraser started the Brackla Distillery in 1812 and distilled illegally. In 1817 he could no longer stay outside the law and was forced to buy a license. Business was going well, although the Captain was not very careful about paying excise duties and other forms of government levies. And so the excisemen were regularly at loggerheads with him.

Nobody knows exactly how and why, but in 1835 King William IV bestowed upon Fraser a Royal Warrant of Appointment, recognition as a purveyor to the court, with all the benefits that entails. Some argue it was just nepotism, but William Fraser didn't listen and immediately changed the name of the distillery to Royal Brackla.

He was the first Royal in the Scotch whisky industry. The new name helped it become a big success. All advertisements explicitly referred to 'The King's Own Whisky', a fact which didn't harm their reputation.

But after a while, the King grew tired of Fraser's persistent indecency (Fraser was convicted several times), and tried to take back his warrant.

Fortunately for Fraser, King William died in 1837 and Queen Victoria kindly extended William Fraser's charter.

QUEEN VICTORIA AND THE NEIGHBOURS

In 1852, Queen Victoria bought Scotland's Balmoral Castle, which she had rented for more than four years. She paid 30,000 pounds. In the years she stayed there, she met her closest neighbour John Begg, who ran the New Lochnagar Distillery just a mile from her home. We know she not only knew him, but she visited him several times with her husband Prince Albert and the children. On every visit, they were welcomed with open arms, and tasted new spirit and some aged whisky before walking back home happy.

Not only was Prince Albert a whisky fan, but Queen Victoria appreciated whisky. According to insiders, she often drank a cocktail of Bordeaux wine and whisky. But a whisky with tea was always welcome too.

It didn't take long before John Begg was awarded a warrant and allowed to change the name of his business to Royal Lochnagar. From that day on, John distilled a special expression, Balmoral whisky, which still stands in the cupboards at Buckingham Palace and the current Queen's country residences.

In 1976, Royal Lochnagar became part of the Distillers Company Limited (DCL). The management decided to omit the 'Royal' prefix everywhere: on bottles, letterheads… everywhere. They were angry. Prince Philip, Duke of Edinburgh, had given a lecture at a party somewhere, stating that those Lochnagar lads were degrading and polluting the whole area of his Balmoral. For almost ten years you could not find 'Royal' on the Lochnagar bottles.

In 1986 they realised their mistake and humbly asked to use 'Royal' again.

GLENURY ROYAL DISTILLERY

Captain Robert Barclay might never become famous for his participation in the Battle of Waterloo. But he had other victories to his credit. He was a celebrated boxer who made a lot of money, and a long-distance walker who could easily cover 100 miles in less than 20 hours.

And he was a distiller. In 1825 he started a distillery in Stonehaven, south of Aberdeen, Scotland. The distillery stopped production in 1983 and was demolished two years later. Now, there is no trace of it, except perhaps for a rare bottle which will certainly cost a lot of money.

It was that same King William IV from our Royal Brackla stories who granted Glenury a royal warrant. They were very close friends.

That was a thorn in Royal Brackla's side, especially when Queen Victoria went a step further after the King's death and gave Glenury permission to call themselves 'Distiller to Her Majesty'.

75

THE ROYAL CRASH

GOOD NEWS FOR LAPHROAIG

The most unforgettable moment in the life of a true whisky enthusiast is when the heavy gate of a warehouse opens and you are invited to enter. It's exactly like entering into the Limbo of Heaven. The penetrating smell of the 'angels' share' and the view of hundreds of barrels full of 'juice of the barley'… It causes a person to be silent.

In one of Laphroaig's warehouses, there is a good chance that you will come across a barrel with 'Charles' written on it in thick black marker.

It is almost certain that this 'Charles' is 'The Prince of Wales'. He has barrels everywhere, but at Laphroaig, you will find his most famous barrel.

On June 29, 1994, the British Aerospace or BAe 146, one of the passenger aircraft in the Queen's fleet, approached the small airport at Port Ellen on the island of Islay. At the tiller was Captain Graham Laurie. Next to him was the heir apparent to the British throne, HRH Prince Charles.

Charles got a pilot's license, but he didn't take it very seriously with the regular training sessions afterwards. Nevertheless, the captain allowed him to ground the plane. At least, that was the intent.

A VIP VISIT

Islay has a runway that is about a mile long. That is enough for the BAe 146. But you have to use the entire strip and not land in the middle of it, like Charles did. Reducing the speed is also recommended, as is taking into consideration the strong tailwinds. Those mini details caused the aircraft (with its 23 tons) to slide at the end of the runway and to drill its nose into the soggy peat floor of the whisky island. The incident caused one million pounds in damage. Six crew members and five passengers escaped unscathed.

In the news, bad weather and burst tires were blamed for the accident. The captain was allowed to stay with the royal fleet, but he was advised to land his planes on his own in the future.

A year later, Charles made it official that he would never do it again. His visit to the Laphroaig Distillery (one of his favourite whiskies, especially the fifteen years old), was planned for twenty minutes, but it lasted several hours, until a new plane came in to pick him up.

As a mark of gratitude for the warm welcome and for the delicious whisky, the prince contributed a royal warrant to Laphroaig. All bottles now bear the Prince's coat of arms with the revealing motto 'Ich Dien': 'You can count on me'.

You will agree, this was an easy way to get the title 'purveyor'. Others had to do more to get it. But Laphroaig is not the only distiller to supply the Queen or the Prince of Wales.

Other whiskies also bear coat of arms or blazon: J&B, Chivas Regal, Johnnie Walker, The Famous Grouse, and Dewar's to name a few.

There are still stories circulating about other distillers in the sector who yearn for such a label. In 1848, the owner of the Ben Nevis distillery had an entire cask sent to Queen Victoria.

But the queen, not at all averse to a 'wee dram', didn't react.

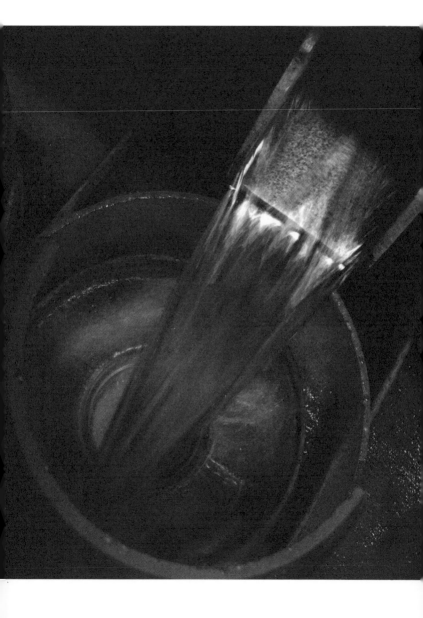

76

THE WATER OF LIFE

AQUA VITAE IS GOOD FOR YOU

Scotland's oldest free lending library can be found in a small town near Perth: the Library of Innerpeffray. It cherishes a large collection of historical books and documents.

One of them, a book printed in 1577, is called 'The Chronicles of England, Scotlande, and Irelande', written by Raphaell Holinshed.

Holinshed worked as a writer-translator in London after he graduated from Cambridge. His 'Chronicles' made him famous. The book had an impact on the intellectual world at the time, even though we now know that it contains a few inaccuracies.

Even William Shakespeare used the Chronicles of Holinshed in the writing of a number of his plays.

We are particularly grateful to Holinshed for writing down what he learned from a man apparently well versed in 'aqua vitae'; the water of life.

'One Theoricus wrote a proper treatise of Acqua Vitae, wherein he prayseth it to the nineth degree. He destinguishe the three sortes: simplex, composita and perfectissima. He declareth the simples and ingrediences thereto belonging. He wisheth it to be taken as well before meate as after. It dryeth up the breaking up of hands, and killeth the fleshe wormes, if you wash your hands therewith. It skoureth all skurfe & shaldes from the head, being daily therewith washte before meales. Being moderately taken, sayth he, it sloeth age, strengtheneth youth, it helpeth digestion, it cutteth fleume, it abandoneth melancholy, it relisheth the hart, it lighteneth the mynd, it quickeneth the spirithes, it cureth the hydropsie, it healeth the strangury, it pounceth the stone, it expelleth gravell, it puffeth away all Ventositie, it kepeth & preserveth the hed from Whirlyng, the eyes from dazelyng, the tongue from lispyng, the mouth from mafflyng, the teeth from chatteryng, the throte from rattling, the weasan from stieflyng, the stomacke from wambling, the belly from wirtchyng, the guts from rumbling, the hands from shivering, the sinowe from shrinking, the veynes from crumpling, the bones from akyng, the marrow from soaking.'

This is how you hear it from someone else.

Woodcut of the brewing process of the water of life.

77

THE SEVEN-DROPS PRINCIPLE

WHAT WE ALL THROW AWAY!

Years ago, I learned something from a Scottish friend about saving money. "Ha, ha...," you will say, "there are those stingy Scots again!" Wrong, it's about thrift in relation to whisky. After an evening of chatting over a dram and proving that a full bottle is too much for one person but too little for two (as the Scottish saying goes), I learned how to handle an empty bottle according to the seven-drops principle.

It's simple: when your bottle is empty, place the bottle flat on the table and wait ten minutes. Then pick up the bottle and pour the contents very slowly into a glass... while counting the drops. Stop at seven drops and put the bottle flat again. Again, wait for a while and then repeat the above. Count seven more drops. You have to repeat it a third time. You will notice that those last drops come very slowly. But anyway: you will get seven drops again. You will have twenty-one drops in total. The experiment ends there.

Yes, of course, there are always people who want to do this a fourth time. Shame, don't do it. Stick to our seven-drops principle. Try it at home. It works.

We investigate the principle frequently. It's the only way to conduct serious scientific research. You will probably be astonished by what follows, but I want you to be aware of it.

We eventually get 21 drops from one empty bottle of booze. Those 21 drops together make up one millilitre of whisky (approximately). Accordingly, ten empty bottles will give us one centilitre of whisky.

And now we are going to look at the statistics! Scotland alone exports 1.3 billion bottles of whisky each year. Once empty, almost all of those bottles are thrown into glass containers. Without applying our seven-drops principle! Hence, with every bottle, one millilitre of whisky is thrown away.

Let's go ahead and calculate: 1.3 billion millilitres of Scotch whisky is simply thrown away every year. This is 1,300,000 litres of whisky or about 1.8 million regular bottles.

Whisky! Thrown away! Terrible!

When will they finally agree to make our seven-drops principle mandatory all over the world?

78

KEEP WALKING ...

LEFT? OR RIGHT?

Take a guess at what it is: a brisk walking man with white breeches, black riding boots, a walking stick with a silver bud, a striking top hat, and a monocle. When you see it in its original version, it's a bit old-fashioned, but nicer and more streamlined in the modern version.

Exactly: Johnnie Walker, the most recognised logo in the whole world. You latched on to the image of a square bottle with a slanted, gold-rimmed label. This is the result of well-thought-out marketing, which has taken more than 150 years of hard work.

It all started around 1870, when the whisky in question was still called Old Highland Whisky and Alexander Walker (Johnnie's son) came up with the idea to make the bottles square, so that they would not only stand out better, but also become stronger and more convenient to pack in crates. He had a plan: he wanted to sell his whisky everywhere a ship could reach. The ship captains were his salespeople: they received his bottles for free, sold them in distant countries and were allowed to keep a large part of the proceeds for themselves. His whiskies conquered the world.

Alexander died in 1885 and his son, Alexander II, continued the business. He changed the name to Johnnie Walker Scotch Whisky. While having a drink with the artist Tom Browne, Alexander suggested the idea of the Striding Man, as a tribute to his grandfather. Tom used a napkin to sketch the picture. It would last 'forever'. A businessman and friend of the Walkers, Lord Stevinson, later linked the famous slogan 'Born in 1820. Still Going Strong' to the picture.

At the end of World War I, you could find the Striding Man in more than one hundred and twenty countries. It was the beginning of continued growth.

In 2000, however, the Striking Man lost his way and, in his sleek and elegant attire, began walking in the wrong direction! To the right, instead of to the left as he had done for nearly a century.

It was just one of the marketing tricks to give the famous whisky a new and even better image: the worldwide Keep Walking promotion. From that point on, the man would walk toward 'the future', toward 'new goals', toward 'progress'...

Johnnie Walker could no longer be ignored by newspapers and magazines and was present at the most diverse cultural and non-cultural events.

Fifteen years later, they gave the campaign an extra push with a 'Next Step' action: 'every step you take should be one towards the realisation of your dreams'.

Something else has changed as well. Anyone who has ever visited a distillery owned by Diageo, the owner of Johnnie Walker, will certainly remember the stern voice of the guide who repeatedly forbade us to take pictures.

But on my last visit, I was almost begged to take as many pics as I could and post them on Instagram, Facebook, and all other social media as soon as possible.

79

GLENCAIRN GLASS
NOT ALL GLASSES ARE CREATED EQUAL

There is a lot of gossip in the whisky world. Go to a whisky festival and discreetly mingle with a group of so-called experts, sniffing glasses, sipping occasional sips, and nibbling and smacking. Then utter words such as 'light and velvety', 'touch of this', 'slight undertone of that', 'the smell of crushed…', and the bitterness of old…', and so on. The best thing to do in that circumstance is to run.

It gets even worse when, without knowing it, you end up in a group of glass experts: those who know in which glass you should consume which liquid. There aren't many, but you can find them everywhere. 'The right glass' is a vital subject in the whisky world.

Whisky aficionados get annoyed when that idiot bartender pours the single malt you ordered into a tumbler and then tosses in a few more blocks of ice, without asking.

The law does not allow killing bartenders, but some say it would be a nice solution.

A tumbler is a good glass for anything that isn't really good enough on its own, so you need to add something else to improve it. When you drink whisky, you use a real whisky glass. And that's it.

Scientists and universities have tackled the problem and tried to find ways to allow the four centilitres in your glass to unfold in a masterful way, to keep the aroma under your nose, and to give you the full one hundred percent of your expensive drink.

And you have a choice: a NEAT Glass? A Nilan Glass? A Tom Dixon Glass? A Malt Glass by the Finnish designer Mikko Laakkonen? A Copita Glass? A Tüath Glass?

OR A GLENCAIRN GLASS?

For years, Raymond Davidson, owner of the glass company Glencairn Crystal near Glasgow, has been annoyed by the fact that his malt whisky was always served in a tumbler at the pub. He decided that he would design a glass that the whole whisky world would like. He tinkered with it for a long time.

When he was satisfied with the result, the drawings disappeared into a drawer. Other assignments took precedence. And soon, he had forgotten his 'miracle glass'.

The world famous Glencairn glass..

Years later, his son Paul discovered the model glass designed by his father and contacted the major distilleries to ask for their opinion. There was great enthusiasm in the field. Paul was eager to take advantage of the comments received and he made some minor adjustments to the proportions and form.

'The' Glencairn glass was born: a glass with a sturdy foot, like a tumbler, and a convex chalice with a narrowed neck, which opens gradually at the top.

It's ideal to fully discover the aromas and flavours of the whiskies.

Before long, most of the distilleries chose the Glencairn glass. However, it didn't end there: Glencairn glasses are used at almost all whisky festivals in the world.

80

LOCH EWE DISTILLERY
SCOTLAND'S SMALLEST DISTILLERY

Another subject that gets talked about a lot: which distillery in Scotland is the smallest? Does this refer to production? The surface? The height of the buildings? The size of the stills?

It's simple though: Scotland's smallest legal distillery was the Loch Ewe Distillery in Aultbea on the northwest coast. And that will always be the case.

Like many whisky stories, this story of Loch Ewe has its roots in tax law.

Although those taxes had been introduced in Scotland as early as 1644, it was not until the Union of the Crowns, in 1707, that the first excisemen—the checkers—travelled to Scotland.

In the south, they forged plans to limit the illegal distilling of those 'barbarians' in the north. The Excise Act of 1823 was the first step: that law reduced the minimum capacity for a still to forty gallons, about one hundred and eighty litres. In 1860, the Spirit Act was even stricter: each still had to hold at least four hundred gallons. One thousand eight hundred litres can't be easily hidden by an illegal stoker.

But the law left a loophole. And, years ago, John and Frances Clotworthy took advantage of it.

THE LOOPHOLE

John was a firefighter at Glasgow Airport. After retiring, he opened the Drumchorck Lodge Hotel, on a remote peninsula in Wester Ross, Scotland. He and his wife, Frances, made a few trips to the United States. They visited several distilleries and there the idea grew to set up their own small distillery, where everyone could distil his own whisky.

They didn't need a large still. They applied for a forty-gallon still. But they were prohibited by that 1860 Spirit Act. John studied that law very closely and discovered one phrase that rang a bell.

The Act specified a possible derogation for 'new projects in regions that are economically less developed'. That was the exact definition of the area where John had set up his small hotel.

The people of Her Majesty's Customs and Excise could not believe their ears when the Clotworthys pointed it out to them. They would have to delete that sentence, and as soon as possible. And they managed to do it, on June 20, 2006.

'They called us that day to report the "sad" news,' John Clotworthy said, 'but we also had some news for them. An hour before the bill was changed, visiting 'excise' inspectors granted us a license for the next one hundred and ninety years."

They faced a fait accompli.

In the garage, behind the hotel, the car had to make way for a German-made still of barely one hundred and eighty litres. Immediately, the news made the front pages of all British newspapers. The 'illegal' Loch Ewe Distillery, with its much too small still, had become big news.

Quick photographers even had a picture of the entire distillery with the washback in the middle where the fermentation took place: a green waste container. On wheels. A rod heater from an aquarium shop was used to maintain the temperature of the wash.

Multipurpose washback in Loch Ewe distillery.

The weekly production of the Loch Ewe Distillery fluctuated around ten litres. Scotland's smallest distillery, however, only lasted a few years. In 2017 the Drumchorck Lodge Hotel had to close its doors. And Scotland's smallest distillery stopped.

Until recently you could find the graceful letters 'Loch Ewe Distillery' above the garage door.

81

MEKHONG WHISKY
THE PRIDE OF EVERY THAI

You can buy a bottle of Mekhong whisky in Thailand for less than five pounds. Rich and poor, young and old. All drink it. Mekhong whisky is not only Thailand's national drink, it is also the pride of every Thai. Mekhong whisky is a monument; an institution. But it is not a real whisky, because it's made of 95 percent molasses and 5 percent rice. The drink is finished afterwards with a secret mixture of herbs and spices. It's more like a rum. And the alcohol content is too low to be whisky as we know it, but in Thailand anything that contains 35 percent ABV is can be considered 'whisky'.

There is no rule of thumb for how to consume this drink. It is either drunk straight from the bottle, or as a 'cocktail': for example, diluted with sparkling water, sometimes with a splash of lemon juice and preferably with a few cubes of ice.

Mekhong whisky, on the market since 1941, was the very first spirit produced in Thailand. In 2010, the name was bought by ThaiBev, owner of virtually all alcohol licenses in Thailand and five distilleries in Scotland, including Old Pulteney and Balblair.

Thai's water of life.

Jokers claim that ThaiBev bought Mekhong because the company couldn't bear the idea that there was another spirit on the market that offered you more headaches than their own SangSom, in ThaiBev's portfolio since 1977.

Like Mekhong, SangSom cannot be called 'whisky'. The bottle also mentions the word 'rum', but it isn't rum. It is a very sweet drink (which is best enjoyed with sparkling water, a squeeze of lemon juice and lots of ice), but it does contain 40 percent ABV. Like its predecessor, it is distilled from molasses and adjusted with herbs. What's more, the neutral molasses alcohol is blended with three-year-old rum aged in oak barrels.

With SangSom, ThaiBev captured seventy percent of the Thai spirit market. And the company has also Hong Thong, a spirit with an equally secret recipe, but also based on rice and sugar cane. The name means 'golden phoenix'. It's a somewhat sticky substance that doesn't just look like cheap cough syrup.

The bottle mentions 'blended spirits' and it contains 35 percent ABV. In Thailand, it's... whisky.

82

GLENMORANGIE HELPS
FORGET THE EMERGENCY NUMBER

Glenelg is a harbour town on the west coast of Scotland, a considerable stone's throw from Skye. The village has about three hundred inhabitants, spread over forty square kilometres. Yet Glenelg is 'world famous'. It is one of the few places in the world that has a palindrome name, which you can also read from the back to the front. Even more: Glenelg uses (in the summer) the last revolving ferry in the world: on arrival, two men (and the dog Nok) turn the loose upper deck on its axis, laying it down on top of the roadway.

Most importantly, Glenelg is twinned with Glenelg... on the planet Mars. NASA chose the name Glenelg to indicate the place where the Curiosity, the robot jeep, would pass twice, once from both sides.

Glenelg has one pub, The Glenelg Inn, where we heard a strange story.

Glenmorangie distillery, a cathedral.

Some time ago, a man from the area was fed up with life. There was no future for him and he got ready to put an end to it. When he had finished securing his noose, he decided, as a last act, to gulp down a good-sized whisky. He opted for a Glenmorangie. And then for a second, and a third...

When he woke up, he found out that he had forgotten to hang himself. He was convinced that it could only be the result of that Glenmorangie. Starting from that thought, he concluded that there was still something worthwhile about this world after all. And he decided to stay for a little while longer.

He sent a thank-you note to the distillery.

He promptly received a package, containing nine bottles of Glenmorangie.

Don't ask me for the man's name, because at The Glenelg Inn everyone had suddenly forgotten all names.

Anyway, let's ask the Glenmorangie Distillery if they know anything about it. Glenmorangie festively labels its bottles: 'Perfected by the sixteen men of Tain'. At least one of these men has to remember this incident. We sent an email and received an immediate answer from Kate Newton. There are also 'ladies' among those 'sixteen men'.

She thought it was a very nice story, certainly not out of place to include in my book. But no one at the distillery could confirm the story.

Back to The Glenelg Inn: only glances of incomprehension.

And a 'dram' each, to prove it's a true Glenelg story.

83

MACALLAN'S SECRET ROOM

THE SOUND OF BOTTLES

Without wanting to offend anyone, a person who has never heard of Macallan might be called a 'whisky layman'. Macallan is a monument from Speyside in Scotland. When I was young (or at least a lot younger), I could tell, eyes closed, how a Macallan whisky tasted, aged as it was in a so-called sherry cask.

Any whisky lover knows what I mean.

But times have changed. Macallan didn't always mature its whisky in sherry casks as everyone believed. Macallan also secretly used a huge amount of bourbon casks.

And the results can now be found in the different expressions that the distillery produces.

The 'secret' room.

Anyone who comes to the distillery today will be astonished: an almost endlessly undulating construction, artfully embedded, hiding in the landscape.

Nostalgic whisky enthusiasts gaze in amazement and search desperately for the unmissable pagoda.

Ah yes, new times, new distilleries.

But leave this building for what it is and walk leisurely to the River Spey. It's a long walk, to an ornate house from 1700: Easter Elchies. It belongs inseparably to the distillery and is therefore on every bottle.

The house, whose foundations may be much older, was built by John Grant of Elchies. In 1820, Alexander Reid, a local teacher, rented the house and the entire property. A few years later, he started a distillery. After thirty years, his whiskies were prominent on every market. His successor, Roderick Kemp, continued production and eagerly experimented with sherry casks.

Strange things must have happened to that man. Since his death, you can still regularly bump into his ghost in the Easter Elchies house.

Fake or real Macallans?

And the house holds another secret, which it doesn't give up easily. The lucky one who gets the opportunity to experience it enters through a small door into a dark, octagonal room with an octagonal sofa set into the floor in the middle of the room, covered with leather-cushioned Chesterfield-style cushions.

Once your eyes get used to the darkness, you'll notice historic Macallan bottles all around you. And only then does an organ start, with part of the percussion consisting of bottles.

You might not believe me, but this puts you in an unforgettable mood, especially with a Macallan 25 years. Tastes great.

Believe me.

84

FAKE WHISKIES

NO ONE IS SAFE

Years ago, I was in a hotel bar on the edge of the Serengeti in Tanzania. In front of me was a bottle of Johnnie Walker Black Label. Next to me was a hotel manager with a set of questioning eyes. The night before, a customer had claimed that the Black Label was a fake. It turned out the claim was true. 'It's pretty much a disease in Africa,' the manager said. 'More Johnnie Walker Red is drunk on this continent than there is made in Scotland.'

At the McDowell Distillery in Goa, India, the master distiller once assured me that half of all the foreign whisky in India was counterfeit. In Vietnam I was asked if I could get them Blue Label bottles. Empty, that is. They were even willing to pay well for it.

There is some tampering with whisky. As long as it stays with that one fake dram, you don't really care. But when it comes to a fake 'rare, old bottle', you, as a collector, not only gain an experience, but you lose a lot of money.

🔻 Not faked, but look-alike.

If you feel the urge to collect bottles, talk to Emmanuel Dron first. He explored whisky in his hometown of Lille and was immediately fascinated by it. He worked at La Maison du Whisky in Paris for thirteen years and started his own bar The Auld Alliance in Singapore in 2010.

The Auld Alliance has become the whisky lover's Mecca. Emmanuel managed to collect a huge number of unique bottles. Many of them are open and can be enjoyed.

But there is more: he also wrote an illustrated encyclopaedia 'Collecting Scotch Whisky', the first volume of which has been published. Carefully take it on your lap (the book weighs more than six kilograms) and discover the easiest way to unmask forgers.

It's not really easy, because the disadvantage of such a questionably expensive bottle is that you actually have to open it to be sure that the contents are real. An open bottle is not worth much.

But the outside can also reveal a lot: the bottle, the label with the type of paper used, the fonts, the printing technique, the inks used, the glue, the language errors... These can all be clues.

Old bottles and paper from the nineteenth century are easy to find. The cork can also reveal a lot, because hanging in alcohol vapor for a century leaves traces on a cork. But corks can also be artificially aged.

The last resort remains the C14 dating, which can be used to estimate the age of organic material on the basis of the isotope carbon-14.

The Macallan distillery clearly experienced this at the beginning of this century. Their whisky is well liked by collectors and if a unique old bottle suddenly comes to the surface, there is a good chance that it is a Macallan.

Around 1990, not one, but a whole series of very old Macallans were up for grabs on the market. The distillery bought about a hundred of them, had them checked by experts who decided that all but a few of the bottles were genuine. Macallan immediately launched the 'replica series', with exact copies of those old gems.

But the rumours started. Newspapers and magazines questioned these 'new' old whiskies. Whisky experts publicly expressed their doubts. In 2003, Macallan decided to have the C14 dating applied to a number of bottles that date from the second half of the nineteenth century. The verdict was harsh: the carbon-14 analysis indicated that the whiskies had certainly been distilled after 1950.

Macallan was the proud owner of many fake Macallans.

85

COPPER BEAUTY
SCRATCHES AND DENTS INCLUDED

For faithful whisky aficionados, there is only one place on earth that has all the hallmarks of the Garden of Eden: the still room in a distillery. They enter it with bated breath, become very quiet looking at all that copper beauty, and admire the majesty of those enormous masterpieces.

There's the grace of the still's bulging belly, the seductive elegance of its tight waist, and the graceful curves of its neck. There's the beauty of the 'lyne arm', high above the still, that folds away and disappears seductively through the wall. In its presence, most fall silent.

The still has the highest cuddliness factor of the whole distillery. But it's better not to touch, since those damn things can be very hot.

To make it even more romantic, the guide will tell you, in a hushed voice, how important those curves in the stills are for the final taste and the development of the whisky. You will learn how copper, as a catalyst, starts reactions between the acids and the alcohol in the boiler to create new fruity esters and how the copper will degrease and refine the alcohol. And how a bit of that copper goes into your whisky, which is good for the metabolism in your body. And how...

It is a form of hypnotism... Back home, when you're already in bed, you will still hear in the distance: 'Copper...', 'Copper...'

The next morning, you will suddenly remember that there was copper in the whiskies you had the night before. And thinking soberly, you have to come to a conclusion: after all these years, losing all that copper, the stills must have become paper thin.

And so they have.

Originally, they were six to ten millimetres, but after twenty years, not very much remains. And in the end, the still leaks.

Part of it must be replaced.

At the distillery, probably already in a dream, you will have heard your guide with their beautiful Scottish — or Polish — accent tell you that the leaking part is taken out and used as a mould for the new piece. The coppersmith makes the new part identical, the same scratches and the same dents as the old one. Otherwise, the taste of the whisky will change.

Wow. That's craftsmanship.

But is it true?

Coppersmiths are master craftsmen. What do you think? Does a coppersmith make dents and scratches in his new piece of art? While visiting Forsyth in Rothes, Scotland, where the vast majority of all stills are made, I didn't dare to ask.

Coppersmiths are big.

But I still don't understand why, in some distilleries, older stills have pieces of copper attached with four rivets.

86

11.11.11
FIRST DROP OF JAPANESE WHISKY

No, I am not talking about that legendary November 11, 1918, when at eleven o'clock that miserable Great War I ended, even though the armistice was already signed at five o'clock in the morning.

Now, we are talking about whisky. About Japanese whisky.

On September 1, 1923, early in the morning, Japan was hit by the enormous Kanto earthquake. 8.3 on the Richter scale. The capital Tokyo, the port city of Yokohama, and other places were wiped off the map. Japan planned to rebuild the capital in a different, safer area. But those plans did not go through.

A month later, Shinjiro Torii purchased a large plot of safer land ten miles south of Tokyo and built his distillery. He ordered two stills at the Watanabe Copper Works in Osaka.

This weathered still provided the very first drops of Japanese whisky.

On November 11, 1924, at exactly 11:11 AM, the very first drops of new spirit flowed through the spirit safe. Japanese whisky was born on 11.11.11.11.

Every year, on the eleventh of the eleventh month, at eleven o'clock and eleven minutes, the Japanese whisky world celebrates. The party is called 11.11.11.11.

And it wouldn't be Japan if that 11.11.11.11 wasn't used to make people aware of how important it is for everyone that Japanese whisky prevails.

87

PAUL THE APOSTLE

'STOP DRINKING WATER...'

To be read in the letter of Paul the Apostle to his disciple Timothy. No, you don't have to read the entire Bible again to check if this is correct. It's really there! I looked it up. In Paul's first letter. His phrasing was slightly different, however. He wrote: 'Do not drink water alone any longer, but use a little wine, for your stomach and your manifold weaknesses.'

It would have been nice if he referred to whisky, but it was too early for that. The winegrowers should be happy with the Bible. I didn't count it myself, but according to 'The Temperance Bible-Commentary 1868' there are 493 references to wine in the Old Testament and 144 in the New Testament. It's free publicity. Theologians argue that 'wine' in the Bible means 'grape juice'. OK, but then I don't understand what happened to Lot (whose wife turned into a pillar of salt) and whose daughters make him tipsy with wine, and committed incest afterwards?

'Stop drinking water' is advice that has been repeated for hundreds of years. For centuries, it was better to drink beer, wine, spirits, and tea than to drink water. Robert Warner was told that he had to pay an extra premium because he didn't drink alcohol when he tried to take out a life insurance policy in London in 1840.

Were beer and gin so safe at the time? We discover surprising paragraphs when we read old history books. Like the one about Frederick Accum, a German chemist who was intensely involved with gas lighting in London and other places. He had another passion too: he worried about the bits and bobs that could be found in food and drink in the nineteenth century.

In his book on 'Culinary Poison' you will find a whole list of drink additives: cockle berry, for example (currently used for motion sickness, which was not very applicable then, but was poisonous), or arsenic: not something that should be in your cookie.

Most common folk drinks were made with toxic ingredients. The only purpose was to encourage the drinker to drink more.

Of course, the government acted. But, as always, with a bunch of half-decent 'Acts'. They didn't accomplish very much because checks were not forthcoming. Occasionally, however, more intensive interventions were made.

In 1872, the Adulteration of Food, Drink, and Drugs Act pointed out the maximum amount of arsenic you could put in a whisky.

Admit it: a big step forward.

It wasn't until hundreds of heavy drinkers died in central England around 1900 that the problem was examined.

88

DUFFTOWN
WHISKY CAPITAL OF THE WORLD

When Sirius Black managed to escape from Azkaban prison, he was spotted (as far as the movie is concerned) near 'Hogwarts Castle' in the town of Dufftown. J.K. Rowling, who invented the whole story, really had no trouble coming up with a fake name for the strange place Sirius Black would appear. Dufftown is as real as London Bridge. It's the beating heart of Speyside. Even more, it is the capital of the entire whisky world.

'Rome was built on seven hills, Dufftown stands on seven stills!' rhymes a very old song.

Indeed, long ago the village (sorry, the city) had seven distilleries; hence the song. Now there are even more (I'm not giving a number, because these days distilleries are popping up all over the place).

Whisky means money (especially for the government) and that makes it possible for each of Dufftown's 1,500 residents to contribute more to the state cashier than any other Brit.

But that does not mean that the city council is very rich. On the contrary. The pride of Dufftowners, the symbol for its Speyside whisky, and the showpiece of the city is about to collapse: the Clock Tower, built in 1839. It's in the middle of the town. You can't miss it. To save the building, the monument was put up for sale in June 2017 for the sum of one pound.

There was only one condition attached to the sale: the buyer had to promise to renovate the whole building. Potential buyers were given twelve months to respond, but no one expressed interest. The city council saw only one other solution: demolish the cursed thing.

But the Clock Tower is a protected monument, category B, and you don't just send a bulldozer to clean the marketplace. There was more to take care of: the tower clock, a simple timepiece to which the inhabitants are very much attached. In the past, that clock was part of the tower of Banff, Aberdeenshire, where a certain MacPherson was hanged around 1700. That MacPherson was a freebooter who took from the rich and gave to the poor. The sentence was to be executed at noon, but the sheriff of Banff, knowing that a petition for pardon had been granted and a messenger was on his way, had the clock set a quarter of an hour ahead so that he could get rid of that hated MacPherson. Out of pure shame, the timepiece was removed and donated to Dufftown. Because so much rainwater had flowed into it, the electric clock was regularly shut down.

Older Dufftowners have lost count. No one can tell you how many times the electric clock stopped in the past. Sometimes for years. The rainwater that often poured in was a great danger to the electric clock. And it was during one of those long periods that the city council asked a clockmaker to crawl up into the tower to see what was wrong.

The poor clockmaker discovered that at the top of the tower, whisky was being distilled for years. An ingenious system with downspouts ensured that smoke and waste could be removed unseen.

In a small town with so many distilleries, almost every retiree carries a ton of whisky distilling knowledge. And it would be a shame if all that craftsmanship was lost. So, the old song is not quite right: 'Dufftown stands on seven stills ... and a few more.'

89

WHISKY, A MAN'S WORLD?

THE LADY OF THE HOUSE SPEAKING

The bottles of the Glenmorangie Distillery clearly state: 'Perfected by the sixteen men of Tain.' Sixteen MEN. There isn't a female hand involved. Whisky is a man's business, meant for a man's world. You only need to enter the distillery to know this is bullshit.

It's true that you run into a lot of men in the whisky industry, but in many cases, the reins of distilleries are in the hands of women. Female master blenders are no longer exceptional. The brand ambassadors who travel all over the world to promote their products are often women who don't shy away from a 'wee dram' and can tell a damn lot about it.

Let's take a look at the history of whisky. We discover that it was not a man's world at all. Centuries ago, women were the ones who made beer and distilled aqua vitae at home, while men were working in the fields or hunting. Maybe men were able to convince their wives that it was healthier outside than inside. And they swapped roles.

We have to wait until 1950 before we find a lady at the head of a distillery in Scotland: Bessie Williamson, who started out as a secretary at Laphroaig and eventually took over the entire business. There were a few women before her in the whisky business, but they didn't receive the same recognition. Bessie was earth-shattering news and her story can be found everywhere, so I don't have to repeat it here. What has happened in the seventy years since?

The Scotch Whisky Association (SWA), the mighty organization of the Scotch whisky industry, defends the interests of its members around the world. The SWA was founded in 1942 and represents 95 percent of Scotch whisky producers. The SWA watches over the individuality of Scotch whisky and legally attacks any infringement against the misuse of the name. It is the global point of contact when the interests of the Scotch whisky export are at stake.

Today, the head of the Scotch Whisky Association is a young woman: Karen Betts. She studied law and history at Saint Andrews University. She was ambassador to Morocco and played important roles at the British embassies in Baghdad, Washington, Brussels, and in the EU. The director of The Keepers of the Quaich is Annabel Meikle, who grew up in the whisky industry.

A man's world? I don't bet a bottle on that.

90

DIET WHISKY
DON'T WORRY ABOUT WEIGHT WATCHERS! DRINK!

Many of you are familiar with Amrut and Paul John. Amrut was the first Indian distillery to sell its malts on the European market using the 10,000 Indian restaurants in Glasgow in 2004. But the Indian brands like McDowell's No. 1, Bagpiper, Old Tavern, Director's Special, Hayward, Black Dog, and Signature are probably not in your whisky cabinet. They are all produced by the McDowell distillery in the village of Bethora near Ponda, in Goa, India. You will not be able to pick up one of these in Europe because these whiskies do not meet the standards set by European regulations.

In India, molasses is widely used in the distillation of alcohol and foreign (often Scottish) alcohol is also added during blending. As a result, they can forget the European market.

But they don't care much: almost half of all the whisky in the world is drunk in India. This is remarkable for a country that has one hundred and seventy million Muslims and more than a billion Hindus. In addition, some of the 29 states have alcohol-free laws.

Because the country imposed sky-high taxes on imported alcohol, the Indians had to take care of production themselves. It works out very well for them: their distilleries produce more than three billion litres per year. McDowell alone distils 15,000 litres per day. According to the distillery's CEO, the majority of that goes to the Indian army and the United Arab Emirates. But the rest disappears into the hundreds of millions of bottles that McDowell releases every year. And the distillery continues to grow: in the list of the fastest growing whisky brands in the world, recently published by The IWSR Magazine, McDowell is listed in the top 25 six times.

MCDOWELL'S NO. 1, DIET MATE RESERVE WHISKEY

In 2006, McDowell launched its diet whiskey: the McDowell's No. 1 Diet Mate Reserve Whiskey. Creative, you have to admit. It is a blended whisky, to which garcinia has been added, intended for anyone who likes to down a whisky, but also thinks about his or her BMI.

Garcinia is made from the dried skin of the Malabar tamarind fruit, grown in Southeast Asia. Garcinia is strongly reminiscent of citric acid, found in citrus fruits: acid with a slightly bitter undertone. It has a very remarkable property: it prevents certain enzymes in our body from converting all the carbohydrates we ingest into fat. Your body draws from its fat reserves.

There's more: your brain gets the message that nothing more needs to be eaten. This reduces the feeling of hunger and makes you put the fork down. Result: You remain thin.

There is clearly a market for 'diet whisky' in India. It also gives you a unique argument to explain at home why you reach for the whisky bottle so often.

91

WHISKY MATHEMATICS

TO LOSE COUNT

You hate mathematics? No problem. You're not the only one.

But I have to tell you this (and I'm sorry): if you are on your way to becoming a fully-fledged whisky expert, there's no other way. You have to master the whisky numerical language.

But it's simple, right?

When we talk about whisky exports, you might think that 'bottle' is the most logical unit: three million bottles, for example. Bottles are of different sizes in different parts of the world. Since 1992, a normal bottle in Europe must contain 70 centilitres. Previously it was 75, as in the rest of the world. However, the European Commission wanted to make a small difference, making the bottles more recognisable for its own market.

Everything in 'litres'? No, too simple.

Case, crate, or box.

We speak internationally of 'cases'. The word is reminiscent of a 'chest', but actually, these days that has nothing to do with it. The idea may well come from 'a chest or box with twelve 75 centilitre bottles'. Because a case is just nine litres, regardless of whether it is a large or small box, with large or small bottles. Nine litres, that's it.

It's only in the Indian whiskey industry that you have to pay attention: their ten-digit system works differently than ours. One hundred thousand is called 'lakh' and it is written as 1,00,000, while one 'crore' is equal to one hundred lakh, so 1,00,00,000. So, one lakh crore is 10,00,00,00,00,000. But that amount of whiskey is not yet being produced.

We are almost there! Now remember this: the alcohol content is stated on the bottles in 'alcohol by volume' or ABV. This is usually 40 percent (mainly on the domestic market). That makes the bottle slightly cheaper than, for example, 43 percent (usually for export, where it may be slightly more expensive). On older or foreign bottles, the alcohol content is shown in 'degree proof'. This is also simple: if it is American degrees, then you simply divide by two: one hundred degrees is fifty percent ABV. If it is English degrees (and luckily, they stopped doing that in 1980), then you divide by 1.75: one hundred degrees is then 57.1 percent alcohol.

Drinking whisky can be so easy.

92

CRICKET AND WHISKY

AND A SOUTH AFRICAN GIRL

Ever attended a cricket match? And were they able to wake you when it was over? 'Cricket is the only sport invented by God Himself to teach mankind the meaning of "eternity".' George Bernard Shaw, the spiritual father of *My Fair Lady*, was not much of a fan of the sport. 'Baseball is better than cricket,' he added, 'it doesn't take that long.' With 'a game for 22 crazies, followed by 22,000 other crazies,' he fully summarized his affinity for 'men in white.'

Cricket! Twenty-two players, only about three of them doing something while the others watch. The game can go on for days, but luckily it is occasionally shut down for afternoon tea.

If you have no idea how cricket works, these are some of the basic rules: the dimensions of the pitch are not fixed. Neither is the time of a match. It could be a few days. With interruptions, of course. Players must also sleep. There are two umpires, but they don't

▲ Andy Watts.

react until the players point out a foul. They make as few decisions as possible. If a player claims that an opponent was 'out', the referee either raises the index finger (meaning 'yes') or shakes his head. The complainant can go.

You won't believe it, but cricket is at the origin of the entire whisky industry in South Africa.

Englishman Andy Watts grew up in Penistone in South Yorkshire. He was a well-known professional cricketer with the Derbyshire County Cricket Club. That brought him to South Africa in 1982, where he had to teach the players of Boland Cricket — 'We are stronger together' — the tricks of the trade. He stayed there long enough to explain the full rules of the game and to seduce a beautiful South African 'meisie'.

He worked as a blender at the Stellenbosch Farmers' Winery (SFW). A technical agreement between SFW and Morrison Bowmore Distillers brought him back to the UK for a six-month tour of Auchentoshan, Glen Garioch, and Bowmore.

'Jim McEwan, who was at the time manager at Bowmore, helped convince me that producing good whisky is not a privilege of the Scots,' Andy said. 'By the way: until the 1980s, almost all grain whisky in Scotland was distilled from South African corn. All we lacked was five hundred years of experience.'

In 1972 the Stellenbosch Farmers' Winery bought a brandy distillery founded by James Sedgwick at Katrijntjesdrift. Sedgwick was a British sea captain who regularly commanded ships between England and India. In 1859, he founded his James Sedgwick and Company Ltd. in South Africa.

It was a name that would disappear for a number of years, but afterwards would be proudly displayed on the facade again by the new owners. After 123 years, James was back.

The distillery not only produces malt whisky (the only one in South Africa), but also excellent grain whisky.

Andy Watts still heads the Sedgwick Distillery and his Three Ships whisky is still his pride. The Distell Group Ltd, as the business is now called, today also owns the Scottish distilleries Tobermory, Bunnahabhain, and Deanston.

Andy's acquired knowledge of the most complex world of cricket must have helped him as a general manager and master distiller.

for a moment), the name Faraday will still be fresh in your mind. Sir Michael Faraday, the
man of, among other things, the electromagnetic fields and the famous 'Faraday cage'. Do
you remember? Although he was a very busy man, he must still have found time to care for
posterity. One of his descendants, Dr David Faraday, revolutionised the whisky world. David
was a chemist at the University of Surrey in Guildford, England.

More than two hundred miles to the west, in the Welsh town of Hirwaun, a group of
enthusiasts gathered at The Glancynon Inn. They toyed with the idea of starting, for the
first time in 100 years, a new distillery in Wales.

The real Welsh Ghwisgi would be made there again. David Faraday was asked to design a
still able to distil more alcohol faster, better, and cheaper, which would also be purer, and
tastier, and higher in ABV.

And all this preferably in one single distillation run.

David must have had some of his ancestor's genius, as he combined a classic pot still with a tall copper column which held 24 adjustable copper plates. The alcohol vapours are sent back down up to three times by these plates. The wash is distilled over and over again to get new spirit with an alcohol level of between eighty and ninety percent. All in a single run of about ten hours. What's more: The new system saves up to forty percent of the energy.

It does look strange: the classic spirit safe is just a big glass jar. There are no faints and no tails. Everything is new spirit.

Penderyn Distillery is, to my knowledge, the only distillery using this kind of still. David Faraday admitted that 'mastering my still is a true art.'

It was the legendary Dr Jim Swan who helped so many distilleries to get started and who knew perfectly how to tune the still for the different types of spirit they had in mind.

A simple spirit safe.

DR. JIM SWAN

THE EINSTEIN OF WHISKY

I first met Jim Swan in Taipei, Taiwan, about ten years ago, at a convention where both of us were supposed to speak. I had never met a man who could say so much about whisky in so few words. Jim was a huge source of original information and radiated the tranquillity that you can only find in a warehouse of a distillery.

He had a good sense of humour, which was priceless for a serious man.

Those who have the fortunate habit of tasting the whiskies from the most diverse and particularly the new distilleries can regularly expect a 'Jim Swan accent'.

Wherever whisky was involved, people would regularly reach for the phone to ask Jim if he knew how to solve a particular problem. What's more, starters pressed for him to guide them through their first steps: Penderyn in Wales, Kavalan in Taiwan, Cotswolds Distillery, The

London Distillery Company in England, Victoria Caledonian in Canada, Clydeside Distillery in Glasgow, Lindores Abbey in Fife, Kilchoman on Islay, Kingsbarns, Nc'nean, Annandale, Gouden Carolus in Belgium, and even Amrut in India.

Jim studied chemistry and developed a very personal view on production and maturing techniques. He developed his own theory, starting with fermentation and ending with well-chosen barrels. More than anyone else, he was convinced of the importance of wood in whisky production.

Jim was the inventor of the famous STR barrels. STR stands for 'Shaved, Toasted, and Re-charred'. He used old barrels. The inside was first shaved, then toasted, and finally charred again. You might say that shave, toast and re-charred has been around in the whisky industry for a long time and ask why this is so special. The answer is that Jim's barrels are unique because they are old red wine barrels. After their STR treatment, they provide flavours and smells that were not known before. In addition, they are so powerful that a very young whisky in a STR cask acquires much more taste and aroma in a shorter time.

Many distilleries have a series of STR casks in addition to their classic casks, although they often give them a different name. Jim Swan passed away in 2017, but the 'Swan effect' will be found in many whiskies for generations to come.

MY PROPERTY
ON ISLAY
WONDERFUL INVESTMENT

I had doubts about whether I should mention this here. You don't know how the government will deal with taxes on property overseas in the future. But a man can't keep concealing it. And so, I admit: I own land on Islay, the Scottish island. It is not huge, and it is located in a rather densely parcelled and swampy area.

But you don't have a lot of problems with the neighbours. My southern neighbour is Japanese. He is rarely there. I have no idea about my other neighbours, except those north of me. That's a Swede. I am aware of this because he planted a flag on his property.

LAPHROAIG®

SINGLE ISLAY MALT
SCOTCH WHISKY

LIFETIME LEASE ON A SQUARE FOOT OF ISLAY

This is to certify that

Mr Fernand Dacquin

is a *Friend of* **LAPHROAIG** and, accordingly, has become the lifetime leaseholder of an unregistered plot recorded at **LAPHROAIG DISTILLERY**.

As a condition of this award, we agree to pay a yearly ground rent in the sum of one dram of Laphroaig, to be claimed in person at the distillery. You'll understand we're not offering heritable ownership or any right to cut peat, farm sheep or extract minerals from the plot - far better to take up your right to a warming measure of Laphroaig.

Upon the Leaseholder's arrival at Laphroaig we undertake to provide a map, with adequate directions for *locating the* **PLOT**, and suitable protective clothing against Islay's rugged weather and eccentric wildlife.

The **LEASEHOLDERS'** Cupboard will contain at all times essential equipment, including: For ascertaining the boundaries of the plot, one tape measure; a pair of wellingtons, size 12, approximately one foot in length.

For the journey to the plot, protective headgear against *low-flying* **GEESE**; a thick overcoat to repel the inclement Scottish mist; a lifebelt and anchor to safeguard against being blown out to sea; one ball of string for securing trouser legs from inquisitive stoats; and a towel for the Leaseholder to dry-off in the event of unwelcome attention from affectionate otters.

No moment is more special than savouring our rugged single malt at its source to the sound of the sea. To do so is to understand why Laphroaig is the most rewarding and individual of all malt whiskies.

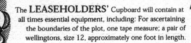

Plot No. _____94591_____

Date ___10, February, 99___

Signed _____.

Iain Henderson, Laphroaig Distillery

A01933

An act to be proud of.

I own property number 94,391 since February 10, 1999. My lot is exactly 30.48 by 30.48 in size. Centimetres. That's one square foot. That makes me one of over a million (as of March 1, 2021) 'Friends of Laphroaig'. All of them have a square foot in a peat field next to the distillery. To become the owner, all you had to do is to buy a bottle of Laphroaig and to send the code number of the bottle to the distillery. Easy. The land remains yours for life, but the distillery rents it back for one mini bottle of whisky a year. You have to ask for it on the spot.

That brilliant marketing stunt was launched in 1994 and today Laphroaig knows its 'owners' in more than one hundred and sixty countries.

But there is nothing new in the world. Laphroaig's marketing man took the idea from a nineteenth-century nobleman who was completely ruined and sold his lands per square foot in order to restore his castle. Crowdfunding 'avant la lettre' converted into customer loyalty.

Honestly, I don't explore my property very often. Although the distillery gives me every opportunity to do so: wellies are ready (size twelve, which is about one foot), rain gear (to protect me against 'any' rain, but also against the geese that attack anyone who is near their nests), and a map.

So, I can go there any time.

Many owners do so. Some propose marriage on their property. Others cut the grass to take home. Ashes have even been scattered and flags have been planted everywhere. The whole world friendly, side by side, on ten hectares of peat land, in the mecca of the whisky world: Islay.

I have to confess something: I would have loved to have had property number one. That lot will always be worth more than all the others. But 'the one' was already taken: by the Duke and Duchess of Rothesay: Charles and Camilla. It's nice to have them as neighbours, but it's a shame that those guys always have the best bits.

How is that possible?

'Foreknowledge!' did you say?

I'm happy to hear you say so. Foreknowledge should be forbidden.

DORNOCH CASTLE
WHISKY CASTLE HOTEL

96

Don't ask a Scot how many islands Scotland has. You trouble that person.

In Scotland, there has been a dispute over the definition of 'island' for centuries (even in the government). For an example: can you call a piece of land or a large rock in the middle of a large lake on one of the islands of Great Britain (an island itself) an island? Not easy to say.

Something else: never ask how many castles they have! Because they have the same problem with 'castle'.

When is something a castle? I don't know. To make it easy, I tacitly estimate the number of Scottish castles to be 'many'. They all have their own history, their own secret room, their own ghosts, and their own stories.

Dornoch Castle, in the cute coastal town of Dornoch, also boasts a ghost. This building was once a bishop's palace from the thirteenth century. After the Reformation, the castle passed into the hands of the Earls of Sutherland. In 1567, the Sinclairs attacked and burned the castle, the whole neighbourhood, and Dornoch's cathedral. Later, in the nineteenth century, the castle was rebuilt and used as a court and as a prison.

There, a guy was convicted for stealing sheep.

The man was devastated till his death and, because of that, is still awake now, a century later. He occasionally wanders around the castle, semi-transparent.

That no one ever saw him can certainly not be blamed on the bar of Dornoch Castle. There are about four hundred whiskies there. Not an earth-shattering amount, but the variety is especially striking: many Japanese whiskies, and a lot of bottles which you can taste which date back to before the war. Whiskybase.com thought this was more than enough of a reason to declare Dornoch Castle Hotel (you can sleep there too) the Number One Whisky Hotel in The World in 2015.

Colin and Ros Thompson, the owners of the hotel, have two sons – Simon and Phil – who have been bitten by the whisky bug. In 2016, they started a new distillery in one of the castle's buildings. This gave Dornoch Castle a very special place in the Scottish whisky lists: I don't know of any other historic castle with its own distillery.

It's an ideal base for people looking for fine whiskies on the east coast of Scotland. This isn't the most spectacular part of Scotland, and it's a long way to go, but at least you have top picks right here at your fingertips: Glenmorangie, Dalmore, Pulteney, and some of the newcomers.

P.S. Because I don't want to leave you forever with the question: what is an island anyway? In Scotland, the definition, which is now almost universally accepted, is as follows: an island is a piece of land, surrounded by water, on which one sheep can survive for one year.

You noticed: Scots are level-headed people.

97

LOMONDIAN CONFUSION

STILL X AND STILL Y

In April 1937 the first pages of Hergé's 'The Black Island' story were published in Le Petit Vingtième. Tintin travels to Scotland; impossible without a splash of whisky. Somewhere in the middle of the story, we find Tintin and Snowy secretly riding on a tank wagon full of whisky on a freight train. 'Johnnie Walker whisky' is written on the wagon. In 1965, a completely redesigned English version was published, in which Johnnie Walker was replaced by Loch Lomond.

And there the confusion begins. Loch Lomond distillery only started in 1966 and the contents of that tank wagon could not have been Loch Lomond whisky. Furthermore, the distillery is not on the 'bonnie, bonnie banks o' Loch Lomond', but half an hour away.

The sexy Lomond Still at Bruichladdich.

But who cares?

In 2001, in the Chinese version of 'The Black Island', Loch Lomond was changed to read 'Scotch Whisky' (in Chinese).

But the Scotch Whisky Association (the SWA, watchdog of the Scotch whisky industry) forbade Loch Lomond from calling their malt whiskies 'Scotch', even though they were made in Scotland.

What was the SWA's problem? Loch Lomond used the wrong stills. Malt whisky must be distilled in a pot still. There are many types of stills: the regular pot still, the Coffey still, the Paracelsus still, the Saintmarc still, the Faraday still, the Adam still, the Lomond still, etc.

Now you think: oh, I see, the Loch Lomond Distillery used the Lomond still.

Wrong.

They used the Saintmarc still (but now a few pot stills as well). The difference is at the top of the still. The Saintmarc and the Lomond still are equally ugly and both have a column on top of the boiler in which there are copper plates to send vapours back down. However, the column of the Saintmarc is much larger than that of the Lomond.

There's one Lomond still at the Scapa Distillery on Orkney, for whisky, and one at Bruichladdich on Islay, for gin. The latter is called Ugly Betty and, until recently, bore the image of a somewhat voluptuous pin-up. The new owners took this away a few years ago.

All that 'Lomond' is very confusing, isn't it? But it will be fine. In the next Chinese version of Tintin, what's written on the tank wagon will be: LOCH LOMOND SINGLE MALT. The Loch Lomond Group is, since the end of 2019, owned by Hillhouse Capital Management: A Chinese company.

ODE TO THE NOSE

BUT DON'T EXAGGERATE

You need all of your senses to taste whisky. Hearing is often overlooked! Uncorking the bottle, that 'pop', is easily underestimated, but it activates the salivary glands and is therefore very important. Just ask Pavlov.

Yes, appearance does matter, and whisky can please the eye, but that can be very misleading.

Accordingly, to discover all the charms of a whisky, we depend on our mouths and noses.

Let's take a look at the mouth. I don't know who counted them, but our tongue is said to have nine thousand lingual papillae. Each papilla in turn has between one hundred and five hundred taste buds and each taste bud also has about a hundred receptor cells! Multiply this, and you will find that we have at least ninety million receptor cells.

Wow!

But how many basic flavours can we distinguish?

Four: sweet, salty, sour and bitter.

Not really anything to be proud of. The Japanese professor Kikunae Ikeda discovered a fifth flavour in 1906: umami (glutamic acid). For centuries, the Chinese have two more: xiang ('aromatic') and xian ('tasty').

But that doesn't help us.

In fact, we only have about thirty different types of taste receptors. Eighty percent are only suitable for discovering 'bitterness'. This is the result of evolution, of self-preservation: many bitter substances are poisonous and therefore worth detecting.

Bitter isn't exactly the first thing we look for in our whisky, although dark chocolate's bitterness can be appreciated in the finish of some whiskies.

From those hideous depictions of the tongue in many whisky books, we learned that 'sweet' is perceived on the tip of the tongue, 'salty' on the sides at the front, 'sour' on the sides at the back, and 'bitter' at the very back of the mouth. That's not quite right: all cells are scattered all over the tongue and in the mouth. Only some places have more of one than the other.

A little experiment: blindfold your partner (first explain the intention, never create false hopes), put a clothespin on his/her nose, and put some cinnamon powder on his/her tongue. Then ask the crucial question: 'What do you taste?' For once, your partner will almost certainly not answer. Remove the clip and the exclamation 'CINNAMON' will be forthright. Take advantage of this happy moment for extensive congratulations, but agree with us: without our nose, we are poor tasters.

VIVA THE NOSE

We need our nose. That is why it is important to exhale through the nose every time we have a sip of whisky in the mouth. But even before we take the first sip, we want to know which aromas can be caught quickly. We hold our nose over the glass and, even if we don't realise it, we let some of that wonderful airflow slide along our 'olfactory epithelium'. You don't have to brag about it. It's not gigantic: two square centimetres on each side. Your dog has ten times more, but fortunately he doesn't drink whisky.

In this epithelium, there are about thirty million receptors — nerve buds — ready to send everything they receive to the brain. The brain compares this information with the content of our 'database of memories'.

Result: a list of possible taste notes, the type you find in numerous whisky bibles, going from 'ground white dead nettle' to 'almost ripe, pale green apples'.

However, there is a small problem here: of all the air we breathe through the nose, only four percent flows past that olfactory epithelium.

FOUR PERCENT!

The rest just passes by. But isn't it incredible that, with such a poor bunch of flawed senses, we can already enjoy so many whiskies? Anyway, I am still left with the same question. When I let my dog sniff my whisky glass with his sophisticated nose, he takes a step back. Does he know something that I don't?

PER MIL

TO SPIT OR NOT TO SPIT

Are you familiar with the image of the 'wine taster'? The wine taster takes a bottle of wine in both hands as if it were their firstborn child. Once uncorked, they take the bottle by the bottom and pour a good amount into the glass.

They take the glass, swirl the wine, close their eyes and let their nose float back and forth over the rim of the glass.

Only now do they take a small sip, letting the wine bounce around in their mouth, and making a jaw movement, as if wanting to rearrange their teeth.

And then they grab a designer trash can on the table and spit all the mess in it.

These images are used in the torture chambers of Scotland Yard to coerce persistent Scottish criminals into confessions. The police officers tell them that they will be given a delicious whisky, but that they will have to spit it out. Such reprehensible practices will bring the most hard-hearted Highlander to their knees. Scots spit whisky backwards.

The rest of the world's whiksy tasting population are always left with the question: 'What am I doing with it? Ingest or spit it out? Ingestion means it will soon get into my blood, with the result that the servant of the law will rip my driver's license.'

Fortunately, I'm still here to help you.

Step 1: you take a big sip of whisky and wait for twenty seconds, asking: 'Swallow or spit?'

Step 2: swallow, because without you knowing it, ten to twenty percent of the alcohol is, through the mucous membranes of the mouth, on the way to your blood.

Step 3: don't panic during this difficult moment, because there is no turning back. On the way to your stomach, about another twenty percent of the alcohol has trickled into your blood.

Step 4: if you get the chance, use the breathalyser. You will notice that traces of alcohol can already be found in your blood. Even if it's only been ninety seconds since you took that first sip.

You will discover the following steps at the next sobriety checkpoint. You can, of course, point out that our body too produces alcohol and that this process is very productive for you. You can prove that scientifically, but I don't know if it helps.

There is one more point: a coffee after a few whiskies does not help at all. On the contrary, it pushes the alcohol level into your blood even faster.

100

TOMMERMÆND
NO, NAY, NEVER NO MORE

You might recognise this: you wake up, and the ceiling appears to have fallen. It's no longer as level as it was yesterday. Your eyes offer you a cloudy kind of David Hamilton effect.

You swallow and it reminds you of that image of the snake eating an entire rabbit. You turn your head to the alarm clock, and it feels like a billiard ball rolling forward in your braincase.

Then you slowly straighten up, your eyes closed, and you speak the legendary words: 'This... is the...last...time! Never again!"

Now you know for sure: you have a hangover. The Danes call it tommermænd, the carpenter. The French call it 'une gueule de bois': a 'wooden muzzle'. Or 'une GeeDeeBee', if it's a chic hangover. There's also a scientific name for it, but since you're already having vomiting tendencies, I'm not going to tell you.

Scientists are more and more convinced that the tastiest things in your drink are responsible for landing the heaviest blows. It is remarkable what your body has to do to process that enormous amount of alcohol and all those congeners.

But I get it: if you're standing in front of the mirror that morning, feeling sick, you don't care what happens inside your body, as long as it happens FAST ENOUGH.

And that's the thorny issue, if I may put it so poetically: to break down ten millilitres of alcohol, your body needs a full hour. Elsewhere in this book, I explained how things work chemically. Just remember this: that's damn SLOW.

Fortunately, you have friends who think they know exactly what you need to do to get back on your feet quickly.

Forget them all. Forget Red Bull, Gammel Dansk (it seems this drink even raises the dead), and Underberg (because it contains as much alcohol as your whisky bottle). Forget cold or hot coffee. Forget tea with sugar.

There is only one solution: first, get to understand your hangover. There are three kinds: a 'biting hangover' makes you puke sick, unmanageable, and almost dying; A 'sluggish hangover' isn't really deadly, but it's annoying, because you don't know if you're going to fall over or not; and a 'false hangover', on the other hand, you don't notice when you get up, but becomes active the moment you want to do something, giving you a cold sweat all over your body, and making you nauseous just as you open the fridge to drink a beer.

In all three cases, only one thing helps: WATER.

Therefore, when you need it most, grab that bottle of water with your left hand (keep your right hand tightly wrapped around the door handle, so you stay upright) and drink! Water saves you!

Although the famous gastronome Jean Anthelme Brillat-Savarin always insisted that chocolate milk was better. But since you swore it was the last time...I don't need to explain that further.

101

BLUFF YOUR WAY
PRACTICE MAKES PERFECT

The worst thing that can happen to a newcomer to the whisky world is that he or she, without realising it, ends up in a group of whisky connoisseurs. One second of inattention can be fatal. The victims usually don't realise it.

It's only when they hear very strange expressions that it gets to them.

Expressions like 'the smell of semi-ripe, southern prunes', or 'smells like wet bicycle handlebars', or 'ideal with the smell of a horse stable', or 'heather after rain'.

What is the best way to act in that situation?

If it's the first time: RUN AWAY.

And then, once home safely, reach for this book and memorise what follows.

You don't have to make it complicated, because basically it's dead simple. There are only two types of whisky: whisky matured in a bourbon cask and whisky matured in a sherry cask. We leave all other barrels out of consideration for the time being, because this is a crash course.

The first whiskies are pale, the second are darker.

Assumption 1

You are offered a pale whisky. Then you use the following terms (not all at once, because you also have to save some for the next emergency). Smell: vanilla, citrus fruits (you choose which one), heather, and honey; Flavour: vanilla cream, almond, coconut, mint, cinnamon, and eucalyptus.

Assumption 2

You are offered a dark whisky. Then you use the following terms (not all at once). Smell: plums, apricots, pears, figs, frangipane; Flavour: cake, hazelnuts, figs, raisins, red fruit (plenty of choice), cloves, nutmeg, and ginger.

You have to spread the different types of nuts very well. Also, don't rumble the words in quick succession, because that creates mistrust. Take a moment between each word. Make it even more colourful, with more words. For example: a whiff of... (if you really don't smell anything), very subtle... (if there's no trace of it), complex, but nicely balanced... (there's a bit of everything in it, but I don't know what it is); a spicy undertone... (this doesn't taste like whisky), and surprising... (they should never have bottled this!).

Never forget to say something about the finish (of course only if you have already swallowed everything): you repeat some of the terms you've learned and conclude with the words: 'dry bitterness'. That's always good. Don't forget: a finish is never 'short', always at least 'half long'.

Of course, you can supplement these basics as you see fit. I've had success many times with 'the fresh morning scent of the bracken', for example. As far as I'm concerned, you can use it.

Yes, of course, you also want to know about the other barrels. Nowadays, many whiskies are 'finished'. The spirit does not stay in a bourbon or sherry cask all the time. After a number of years, the whisky is poured into a rum or Madeira cask, or a wine cask, to create new flavours.

Then, of course, it gets harder! But don't panic: usually it is also indicated which barrels were used for the finish. You just don't have to go into that. It is best to respond as follows: first smile suspiciously, but not too outspoken, so you show that you are not really in favour of tampering with the barrels. Only experts have doubts about this. Never act disdainfully. Just taste it and when you've drunk the whisky, ask casually: 'What would that whisky actually taste like, if it hadn't been finished?'

You'll score with that.

Voilà...

And now, time for practice. Have a whisky...

EPILOGUE

This book matured longer than most whiskies. Many of these stories had been waiting for years and years in my cluttered and overflowing card tray. Some were half written. Others were just a few words. Many of those notes will never turn into a story. Others immediately presented themselves as embryonic narratives and ended up in the pile next to the box. And in this book.

It is not possible to cite all the people, places, events, museums, libraries, bars, distilleries, books, newspapers, or magazines that informed this work. But I am very grateful to each of them. In addition, I have to thank my friend and frequent travel companion Jan Bresseleers for his help and advice from the very beginning of my journey to create this book.

Fernand Dacquin
September 9, 2021
Ghent

www.lannoo.com

Register on our website and we will regularly send you a newsletter with information about our latest books as well as interesting, exclusive offers.

Text: Fernand Dacquin
Graphic design: EHBOntwerp
Typesetting: Keppie & Keppie
Photography: Fernand Dacquin: all, except Shutterstock: 22, 41, 60, 86-87, 102, 124, 130, 157, 192, 230 / Wikimedia Commons: 30, 33, 37, 40, 94, 98, 113, 114, 116, 132, 144, 153, 167, 198, 214, 217, 256, 259, 260, 276, 311 / Wivine Vernieuwe: 46, 190, 234, 339, 341, 343 / Dr Macro: 61, 62, 64 / Kavalan Distillery: 176 / Buena Vista Winery: 92, 93 / Hergé-Moulinsart 2013: 100, 101 / Shannon Tofts: 110, 145, 146 / Ralph Steadman: 126, 129 / Lost Clock Productions: 148 / Firmin Lemaître: 151, 163, 338, 345, 349 / Stefaan Lesage: 168 / William Grant & Sons: 196 / Glenfarclas Distillery: 80, 159 / James Sedgwick Distillery: 318-319 / American Whiskey Trail: 219, 220 / Archive.org: 48, 49 / City of Vancouver Archives: 71 / Clyde Maritime: 88 / Banknote index: 89 / Welcome Library London: 122 / National Galleries of Scotland: 144.

If you have any comments or questions, please contact our editors:
redactielifestyle@lannoo.com

© Fernand Dacquin & Uitgeverij Lannoo nv, Tielt, 20211
D/2021/45/622 – NUR 440, 447
ISBN: 978 94 014 7958 5